BARRACKS TO BUNKERS

250 YEARS OF MILITARY ACTIVITY IN SUSSEX

PETER LONGSTAFF-TYRRELL

SUTTON PUBLISHING

Sutton Publishing Limited
Phoenix Mill · Thrupp · Stroud
Gloucestershire · GL5 2BU

First published 2002

Copyright © Peter Longstaff-Tyrrell, 2002

Title-page photograph: Patchwork repairs to a
barrack block at RAF Tangmere were still
evident in the mid-1990s. This photograph was
taken over fifty years after the building was
struck during a raid by Bf109Fs in 1941 that
demolished a barracks. (*Gote House)*

British Library Cataloguing in Publication Data
A catalogue record for this book is available from the
British Library.

ISBN 0-7509-2908-1

Typeset in 11/13.5 Photina.
Typesetting and origination by
Sutton Publishing Limited.
Printed and bound in England by
J.H. Haynes & Co. Ltd, Sparkford.

OTHER BOOKS BY PETER LONGSTAFF-TYRRELL

That Peace in Our Time
The artefacts of WWII in Sussex
ISBN 0-9521297-0-1 (1993)

Operation Cuckmere Haven
An investigation into military aspects of the Cuckmere Valley
ISBN 0-9521297-1-X (1997)

A Sussex Sunset
RAF Pevensey and RAF Wartling, 1938–1964
ISBN 0-9521297-2-8 (1998)

Tyrrell's List
The Artefacts of Two Great Wars in Sussex
ISBN 0-9521297-3-6 (1999)

Destination Fowington
East Sussex military airfields & Allied aircraft incidents
ISBN 0-9521297-4-4 (1999)

Front-Line Sussex
Napoleon Bonaparte to the Cold War
ISBN 0-7509-2592-2 (2000)

The Seaford Mutiny of 1795
The Royal Oxfordshire Militia Rebellion
ISBN 0-9521297-6-0 (2000)

CONTENTS

INTRODUCTION

This presentation of Sussex fortifications, defence works, sites and structures, artefacts, memorials, curios and collections blends with the evolving history of the county. The contents cover 250 years of military intrigue and activity around Sussex.

My interest in researching and presenting the material within these covers has been praised by amateurs and authority alike. Sourcing fresh information, and putting matters into their correct context for general readership, is an on-going challenge. Knowledge of a wide range of military issues is becoming increasingly appreciated as interest in the county's history becomes more widespread.

Despite official awareness of numerous military sites, and of their historical importance, many military landmarks are still being lost amid urban and rural development. But it is not just in Sussex – there is a similar lack of attention at national level.

Many people have an abiding fascination with underground retreats, whether for civilian or military usage. This book includes previously unpublished accounts of official bunkers around Sussex. Such hide-outs are becoming increasingly inaccessible as time and climatic conditions take their toll, rendering access less and less likely. Additionally, knowledge of these subterranean sites is generally being eroded with the passage of time and records are being lost.

Included on pages 82–5 is a comprehensive doodlebug diary of the V1 attacks on Sussex, together with a Terms & Abbreviations section, to aid general readership. At the start of the twenty-first century this cross-section compilation of the historic defences of the county is intended to be a poignant and seminal statement for public record.

Peter Longstaff-Tyrrell
November 2001

1
The Napoleonic Period

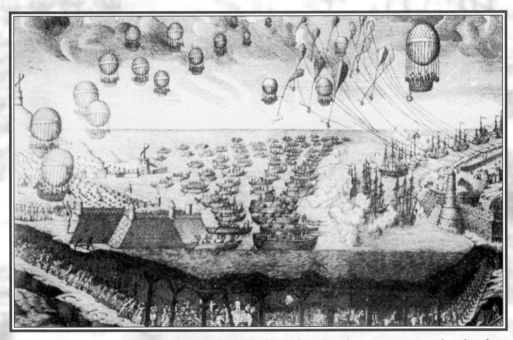

French fervour for the invasion of Britain heightened as Napoleon Bonaparte, who already ruled half of Europe, amassed 130,000 troops and 2,200 flat-bottomed boats around Calais in 1804. A French cartoonist's version of the invasion plan is illustrated in this imaginative portrayal of men being ferried across the Channel by barges, armoured boats and balloons. Creatively they even conceived a Channel Tunnel!

In 1803 Napoleon ordered the Bayeux Tapestry to be taken to Paris to stimulate enthusiasm for the coming invasion of Britain. He even struck a medal in advance, commemorating the successful crossing of the Channel by his troops.

Some years later, in 1815, during his retirement, Napoleon was questioned about the invasion plans by Sir George Bingham, who enquired where the French were to have landed. Napoleon responded that the principal invasion force would have landed between Margate and Deal to forge forwards to Chatham and march on London. (*Eastbourne Redoubt Museum*)

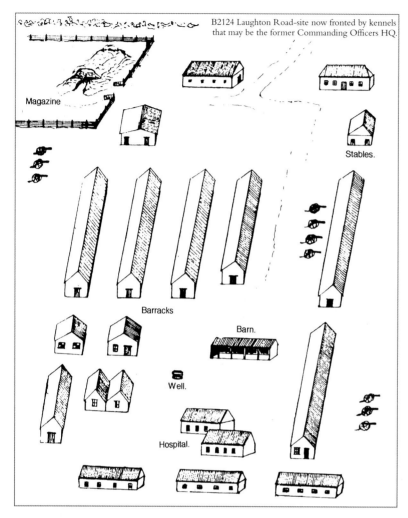

B2124 Laughton Road-site now fronted by kennels that may be the former Commanding Officers HQ.

Magazine

Stables.

Barracks

Barn.

Well.

Hospital.

In 1796 some 50 acres of meadowland at Ringmer, east of Lewes, became the site of artillery barracks, centrally sited to protect the coast. As many as 276 men and 92 horses could be quartered here, and 1,400 barrels of gunpowder were stored nearby. The site soon became surplus to requirements and was sold off by 1828. The timber-clad B2124 roadside former officers' building became Ringmer Lunatic Asylum until 1855, when it was closed down. More recently kennels have occupied the site. (*Gote House*)

Iden Lock on the Royal Military Canal near Rye, 1990s. The former officers' quarters (seen here) and a small barracks nearby are now in use as private accommodation. (*Gote House*)

The prevailing image today of the south coast as an area primarily concerned with leisure, light industry and farming is a far cry from the general situation 250 years ago. The region then was largely occupied by humble artisans engaged in traditional trades and retailing, together with nautical and rural-based industries. Many others were employed on the numerous large country estates.

The Sussex coast had been a target for invaders for centuries. However, it was not until the outbreak of the French Revolution in 1793 that the matter of defence works in the area was adequately addressed by the British government. French attempts to land in Ireland in 1796 and 1798, and at Fishguard in 1797 (troops actually came ashore briefly) raised the possibility that the mainland *could* be invaded. As a consequence of these attacks men of the English working classes were recruited as Volunteers, Militia and Yeomanry Corps – a pragmatic form of Home Guard resistance.

Mid-1750s records indicate that a typical battery was created on a rocky spur just east of the Arun estuary at Little Hampton, although when the threat of invasion receded the property fell into disuse. At the turn of the nineteenth century Napoleon Bonaparte seriously threatened our shores and in 1803 Captain R.S. Bate with four officers and troops manned the rebuilt Little Hampton fort as the county mustered 5,859 Volunteers. A little-recorded branch of defence manning emerged in the form of the Sea Fencibles of the 1800s. Volunteer fishermen, boatmen and sailors were paid a shilling daily, under the jurisdiction of a Royal Navy officer. The coast from Beachy Head to Emsworth was guarded by just 6 officers and 440 Volunteers, spawning the rapid creation of barracks and batteries.

SPASMODIC COASTAL ATTACKS

When the French threat lapsed it left the British mainland with a curious assemblage of redoubts and barracks. Yet French privateers saw no cause to relax their attention to our coast. Parry's 1834 volume *Coast of Sussex* quotes a news report from Brighton on 26 August 1805: 'A French privateer secreted herself last night near Worthing, and about four in the morning captured a sloop laden wih sugars, teas, etc., valued at £7,000. As some of the inhabitants were stirring at early hours they gave alarm and Captain Remus, a revenue cutter, recaptured the sloop about five and brought her into Shoreham harbour. The privateer was captured three hours later and was safely brought into Little Hampton.'

Between 1816 and 1835 HM Customs and Excise mounted an extensive blockade to counter the illicit free trade of goods across the Channel. The Royal Navy Coast Blockade Service, with responsibility for the coast between Sheerness and Chichester, consisted at its height of 3,000 officers and men, with 350 stations between Camber and Beachy Head.

The costly Crimean War of 1854–6, in which Russia was inconclusively engaged in combat with Turkey, France and Britain, dispelled some French animosity as they became our uneasy allies for a time. But Napoleon III was still voicing threats of attack on the British mainland and a schedule of defence was created by the British government of the day.

At the close of 1856 five massive Lancaster guns were shipped from Woolwich for the western battery at Little Hampton, manned by Crimean War veterans. The mere presence of the battery may have served to counter French attention, but in reality the fort hosted only modest numbers of troops engaged in rifle practice across a pair of adjacent ranges, where the golf course now offers another form of contest. By the late 1860s the western Little Hampton fort was manned by a solitary sergeant and a few men. In January 1891 Royal Artillery troops moved the Lancaster guns away and left the fort to deteriorate.

ACCOMMODATING THE NEED TO DEFEND

Debates on the need to fortify the coast of Sussex and Kent intensified from the mid-eighteenth century, headed by the Royal Navy, Army commanders and the Board of Ordnance, politicians and the monarchy. Traditional gun gardens sited at coastal communities were largely redundant, or outdated at best.

Batteries replaced the gun gardens from 1759 when the Board of Ordnance sanctioned the development of fortifications along the coast. Ultimately the programme of defence works was led by Frederick, Duke of York, as the head of our armies and then by William Pitt, who became prime minister in May 1804.

Newhaven Battery consisted of five 12-pounder guns, a magazine and barracks on Castle Hill, west of the 1860s Palmerston Fort which in time absorbed the battery. An earlier lunette battery, on the harbour's western side, supported the unit. Blatchington Battery comprised five 24-pounders, a magazine and barracks and was used until 1870. The late nineteenth-century residential development of Queens Park Gardens at Seaford eclipsed the military installation there. Seaford Battery was less well sited on the beach fronting the town, but it, too, had five 24-pounders, barracks and a magazine. This battery succumbed to the tides and was lost by 1860.

Priority was paid to the 15-mile expanse of vulnerable low-lying terrain east of Beachy Head. The Crumbles shingle, east of Eastbourne, was seen as prime invasion territory and a pair of forts were established there by 1795. Each was armed with six 24-pounder guns firing shot. The western fort was sited on the shingle between Martello Towers nos 69 and 70. The eastern fort was redeveloped in 1850 as Langley Fort, where the Marina now accesses the English Channel between extant towers nos 64 and 66.

The programme of barrack building included a pair of timber-clad units on either side of the exposed Cuckmere River estuary. Records and surviving earthworks at Pevensey Bay and east of Rockhouse Bank at Norman's Bay, at Cooden and around Rye and Winchelsea are testament to the construction of emergency installations.

THE MARTELLO TOWERS CHAIN

While coast batteries had replaced the earlier gun gardens at Brighton and Rye, many eighteenth-century batteries were themselves soon supplemented by the chain of Martello Towers hastily erected, after great debate, from 1804. Construction of the towers, located at 600-yd (firing range) intervals from Rye to Eastbourne – with the later addition of no. 74 at Seaford – was a monumental task at the time. A similar line of towers ran in a southerly direction from Aldeburgh in Suffolk.

Enthusiasm for the financial folly that was the 30-mile-long Royal Military Canal, from Shorncliffe Barracks near Hythe to Rye and then Pett, was surpassed by fervour for the Martello Towers plan. Construction was finally agreed after the 1803 invasion scares, with works commencing in March 1805. By the close of 1806 only seventeen of the

The early 1850s lunette battery at Newhaven retains its original layout, as seen in this view from the 1860s Palmerston fort that superseded the 1759 Cliff and Upper batteries. (*Gote House*)

Although it has been left open to the elements, these unpreserved Newhaven Battery artefacts show evidence of its role in defending the nation. (*Gote House*)

By 1938 Martello Tower no. 65 had been dramatically lost to sea erosion, which undermined its foundations. The chain of towers was inspired by Mortella Point in the Bay of Fiorenzo on the island of Corsica. In 1794 a fortified stone tower with a single 6-pounder and two 18-pounder guns withstood a heavy British bombardment from HMS *Fortitude* (74 guns) and HMS *Juno* (32 guns). Both vessels withdrew after suffering considerable damage and sixty casualties. The enemy tower finally succumbed after two days of attacks when a fire drove out the occupants. (*T.R. Beckett Ltd*)

Tower 64 in sound condition on the Crumbles at Eastbourne, 2000. The brick and stone block tower is scaled off and is afforded no maintenance. Little is known about the Second World War gun emplacements and observation posts found on top of many of these towers. (*Gote House*)

twenty-three towers between Hastings and Eastbourne had been completed, owing to winter stoppages. Each tower was to be armed with a single 24-pounder gun.

Tower no. 1 was at Folkestone, and they were numbered from east to west, up to no. 74 at Seaford – where the conical brick tower was finished in 1812, well over budget at £18,000. With their 'upturned flowerpot' pattern, the brick towers stood almost 33 ft high, with a base axis of 45 ft by 42 ft rising to 29 ft by 35 ft at the top. Walls some 12 ft thick faced the sea and were later rendered to keep out damp, while those on the landward side were just 7 ft thick. Parapet coping was created from Bramley Fall stone quarried from Yorkshire millstone grit. A brick and stone base was sunk almost 9 ft below ground level on the seaward side. Initially entry to the towers was by way of a wooden ladder, 11 ft up from the ground.

Two centuries later many of the forty-seven towers between Rye and Seaford have been lost to the sea or felled by artillery practice. Many people benefited from the towers' robust construction, including contractors and suppliers, as well as workers engaged on their protracted erection. The schedules dominated local building resources for many years.

SUSSEX BARRACKS, 1793–1880S

Records are scarce, and of variable quality, but great care has been taken in compiling this brief account. It is based on Ann Hudson, *Napoleonic Barracks in Sussex*, Sussex Archaeological Society Collections 124 (1986), pp. 267–8. **Aldwick**, see plan below. The *Hampshire Telegraph* in late November 1803 reported the location of barracks. In 1808 troops here suffered from opthalmia. Barrack Yard, **Angmering**, is noted in 1800. The two-storey flint cottages were knocked down between the world wars. There is some doubt whether the 1794 **Arundel** barracks at Crossbush for 54 cavalry were actually erected then, although in 1800 Crossbush barracks for 350 men and cavalry officers is mentioned. Construction from 1804 is recorded and by 1808 the barracks were occupied.

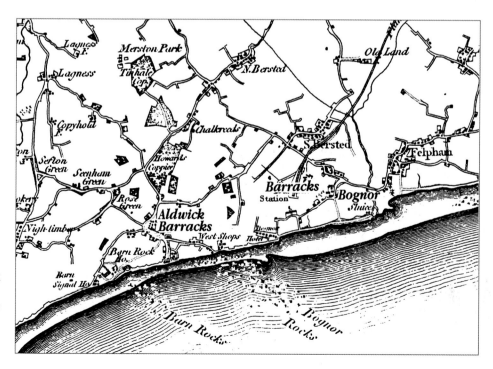

Bognor district, late 1880s. This period electrotype plan shows Aldwick barracks, as well as another barracks south of South Bersted station. (*Gote House*)

Barn Rocks, see map on previous page. In 1798 mention is made of 80 infantry at **Bognor** and **Selsey**. Permanent barracks for 40 men were retained in 1800, but by late 1802 only small barracks remained. In 1798 barracks were built near **Battle** but in early 1800 only temporary barracks for 900 infantry and 120 horses remained. In mid-1803 900 infantry were housed there and in 1806 three stables were lost in an ammunition explosion. The name Barracks Field in Whatlington Road, Battle, is one of several local pieces of evidence helping to perpetuate the history of soldiering in the area.

There is ample evidence in place-names at **Bexhill** for troop activity. In 1798 barracks were built to take 20 cavalry and 500 infantry, and in early 1800 temporary units for 900 infantry and 50 horses were retained. In 1804–5 the King's German Legion was housed here in barracks or wooden huts. Notes state that 3,000 men were housed in huts built around mud-pounded timber frames, with heather or thatched roofs. In 1811 notes mention artillery stables for 100 horses and stores for the King's German Legion. **Blatchington**, see East Blatchington. At **Bognor**, barracks on the site of the later Bognor police station were built in 1805 in six weeks. The buildings had brick foundations, prefabricated wooden walls and slate roofs. The next year one battalion was accommodated here. In 1805 opthalmia struck the camp, which by then had its own hospital unit. The last mention of the barracks in local burial registers came in 1806.

Military occupation at **Brighton** has been amply recorded in literature, verse, song and national archives. Various short-term units took over property round the old town area of the regal resort from 1793. By March 1798 some 300 infantry were housed here and in early 1800 temporary barracks for 660 infantry remained. The main barracks were sited alongside the Lewes Road, initially as Preston Barracks, where the War Office units remained towards the twenty-first century. **Broad Oak** (Heathfield). White rendered cottages facing the A265 retain the name The Barracks.

PRO files mention small temporary barracks at **Broadwater**, Worthing, in early 1800 that were to be given up. From mid-1803 cavalry barracks existed on the Broyle at **Chichester**; initially they housed 1,500 men. The site is better known today as Roussillon Barracks and is the home of the Royal Military Police. During 1814–15 accommodation was found for 888 infantry and 48 officers, plus 328 cavalry with 16 officers and 340 horses.

Cottages built after 1803 in Brook Street, **Cuckfield**, were named The Barracks, indicating some form of army occupation. Short-term timber barracks were built on

The popular Tiger Inn at East Dean, near Eastbourne, once served as militia barracks. Troops would muster on the green outside the picturesque flint building. (*Gote House*)

either side of the **Cuckmere** estuary, east of Seaford, in about 1803. They stood close to the extant Coastguard Cottages. Almost 200 years later foundations of the camp erected near Foxhole Farm could be observed. The site comprised four soldiers' huts, two officers' units, a pair of magazines and the barracks-master's house. By 1814, however, the exposed barracks were dismantled and the huts were sold off. **East Blatchington** barracks have disappeared beneath urban Seaford. They were erected from 1794 of wood with brick foundations. In April 1795 some 500 troops of the Royal Oxfordshire Militia there staged a mutiny (see pp. 16–17). In March 1798 there was accommodation for 600 infantry. In early 1800 permanent barracks for 923 infantry with 57 horses was retained. The barracks were occupied on a reduced basis in 1811 and remained intact in 1835.

Eastbourne and **Langley Point**. Cavalry barracks in the town became a workhouse and were later utilised as part of St Mary's Hospital until redevelopment resulted in demolition of the property. There is mention of temporary barracks in South Street and troops being housed in the seafront circular redoubt. At its peak in early 1800, barracks for 65 rank and file, 4 officers and 24 horses were to be relinquished, but permanent cavalry barracks for 218 men and 63 horses were retained.

Eastergate census records in 1851 mention no. 33 as Old Barracks, **Hailsham** – a triangular plot bordered by London Road and Summerheath Road is recorded in army use. In October 1803 barracks for 1,000 men are mentioned as being built near the present Grenadier Inn and Hailsham Common. They were still in use in 1811 but closed in 1815.

In historic **Hastings** various sites were used as army barracks from 1793. Infantry barracks at Bo-Peep, to the rear of St Leonards & All Saints rectory, and stables close to the top of the High Street were taken over as barracks. **Halton** village barracks were a soldier's mile from the coast and **Fairlight** in 1803 had its own barracks detachment. In July 1794 there were short-term infantry barracks for 199 men at Bo-Peep, with 347 men stationed nearby. New barracks for 54 cavalry troops were under construction. In 1797 grounds at Halton were sold to the government for barracks. In 1798 barracks for 512 men are noted at Hastings, but in January 1800 temporary barracks for 600 rank and file were to be relinquished. By June 1803 no barrack facilities are noted for Hastings, until new barracks were built at Fairlight. In 1804 Bo-Peep barracks were destroyed by fire. In 1823 the Halton barracks were reportedly sold and dismantled.

Horsham and Horsham Common. In 1791 temporary barracks for 2,000 infantry were found in nine timber units, each with cooking and living areas on the ground floor. Accommodation included 60 soldiers sharing bunks on the upper floor. The roof was covered with pantiles. In November 1796 2,000 troops of the national army reserve were stationed at Horsham. In February 1800 temporary barracks for 1,740 infantry were retained, but two years later the *Hampshire Telegraph* stated that only the barracks-master and his family were there. Another report from June 1803 mentions accommodation for 2,400 infantry at Horsham. By 1815 the barracks complex was declared redundant and was demolished.

The 1850s **Kingston** Redoubt at Shoreham, built on a shingle spit at the western arm of Shoreham harbour, has suffered with the passage of time, but generally remains intact. The fortress was partially restored in 1986 and is due to be the subject of Adur District Council remedial attention from mid-2002, with a visitor and information centre planned for the vulnerable site. Construction of a 1940s gun battery here meant the demolition of the defensible barracks on the site.

Langley Point East Fort and Langley Point West Fort of 1795 were replaced by the larger Langley Fort of 1855. In September 1801 two militia companies were stationed at the Langley batteries. In June 1803 accommodation for 70 infantry was found at Eastbourne and Langley. However, *The Times* reported, perhaps erroneously, that temporary barracks for 10,000 men were being erected on Eastbourne beach, with another larger assembly near Pevensey harbour. This news report appears vague to say the least as Pevensey has never had a harbour as such.

The 1797 barracks at **Lewes** occupied a 4-acre site south of Haredean Spring (Winterbourne), north of the Brighton–Lewes coach road. Until a few years ago a modest single-storey cottage named The Barracks remained near the Newmarket Inn, but it could not be found in mid-2001 and may have been replaced by a modern bungalow. The 1797 Lewes barracks were built to the scale of the vast Horsham camp, but were of about half the size and accommodated six troops of men. In 1797 the infantry barracks were completed and cavalry barracks were built alongside. In 1800 accommodation for 1,264 infantrymen was to be retained. Then in 1803 all-new barracks were built at Spital Hill, Lewes, close to what is now the prison. The buildings were planned to take 1,000 infantry, plus 450 cavalry. Units were built of brick and wood with tiled or thatched roofing. Men were housed in 52 small buildings, with 24 men in each. Construction was said to be substantial and superior to that of most cottages, and many units resembled small houses on the outskirts of London. What the men stationed there thought about them is not recorded. The new Lewes camp included officers' quarters, an armoury, a hospital, a canteen and stabling. In 1804 extra barracks for another 1,000 soldiers was reported in the press, with additional artillery barracks added the following year. However, by 1815 the whole site had become redundant and was sold off, reportedly fetching just £3,000 in salvage values.

In June 1794 temporary barracks for 189 infantrymen are recorded at **Little Hampton**. A home close to the beach was converted to barracks. In 1798 barracks for 80 men existed. By January 1800 barracks for 180 rank and file was to be relinquished. In September 1803 barracks for 400 men were being built. These are believed to have stood partly under the Channel Keep flats in Western Road.

PRO files from June 1803 indicate accommodation for 200 infantry at Blatchington and **Newhaven**, plus 55 cavalry at Newhaven and Seaford. A neat row of brick-faced terraced cottages alongside the A22 High Street at **Nutley** are named The Barracks.

Reports on barracks in **Pevensey** may be confused with those in Eastbourne and Langley Point. *The Times* in mid-August 1803 states that a large infantry barracks was being built near **Pevensey** harbour. The following year press accounts said that some 2,000–3,000 men were located there. However, there were no reports of troops at barracks inland at Westham village. Barracks Cottages at **Poling** have been demolished, but were used by troops from Arundel.

Records relating to **Preston** barracks are generally noted under Brighton. From 1795 substantial brick foundations were laid for weather-boarded barracks. In 1800 permanent quarters for 169 cavalry and 215 horses was noted. In 1801 temporary stables for 1,200 horses were erected in the barrack yard during exercises. In June 1803 some 670 cavalry were housed in Brighton. In 1835 625 cavalry rank and file were stationed there. Army occupation of the barracks complex continued well into the 1980s when areas were largely sold off for retail park outlets.

Ringmer artillery barracks were erected in 1798 for troops moved over from Lewes. In February 1800 the interim barracks for 130 infantry and 136 horses were retained. PRO files mention Ringmer barracks in 1802 and 1803 (see p. 6). Records from 1827 state only one troop of horse artillery as remaining at Ringmer, with room for many more. In 1827 the site was largely demolished and sold as salvage. However, the timber-clad officers' quarters alongside the B2124 survive. They have subsequently been used as a lunatic asylum, until 1855, and currently as kennels, along with neighbouring brick buildings that are thought possibly to have been barracks kitchen and hospital units.

In mid-1794 soldiers' acommmodation was found in the converted Great Warehouse at Strand, **Rye**. Temporary barracks for 110 men are recorded. Then in January 1800 temporary barracks for 504 rank and file were relinquished and in 1802 the lease of the Great Warehouse was given up. PRO files show there were no local barracks in mid-1803, although there were suitable sites at Rye and Playden Heights. In 1806 some 168 cavalry and 9,434 infantry were in temporary barracks locally. In 1835 the hospital of **Playden** barracks remained as a private cottage.

Between March 1798 and June 1803 modest barracks accommodated soldiers stationed at **Selsey**. The site of the new 1803 barracks east of Selsey peninsula has now been lost to the English Channel; they housed 16 officers and 330 men, a hospital for 50 and stables for 20 horses. From 1793 **Shoreham** had militia barracks for 386 infantry. By 1814 the barracks had not been occupied for some years. At **Silverhill**, near Salehurst, 1798 reports state that the barracks for 4,000 men were built in eight weeks. It was the largest barracks complex in the county. PRO files for 1800 show interim barracks for 2,048 infantry were to be kept on and in June 1803 barracks there housed 2,100 men. The stores depot was removed after 1815. In 1808 some 4,000 men from the region's barracks were struck by opthalmia. Old Cottages in Kingston Lane, **Southwick**, near the rectory, were reportedly used as barracks. Rectory House was let as barracks around 1800. In 1794 a tithe barn had been adapted as barracks and in June that year some 386 infantry were housed there.

Barracks at **Steyning** are recorded near the parish's southerly limits, in Jarvis Lane and Castle Lane. One report states that in 1792 there were barracks at Steyning, but PRO files from mid-1803 state there was no local barrack accommodation. Around 1804 a large infantry barracks was noted as being erected at Steyning, but this was demolished by 1819.

Barrack Square near **Winchelsea** church reputedly takes its name from the Napoleonic period barracks in the town. In 1793 militia were housed in a former factory. In mid-1794 barracks for 288 infantry existed, but by January 1800 the temporary barracks were given up. PRO records from 1806 mention interim barracks for 31 cavalry and 144 infantry, plus another 408 infantry. Brief inclusion of barracks in High Street, **Worthing**, has been found, but in January 1800 the temporary barracks there were given up. The premises later became the Free School.

NEW BARRACKS

Before the barracks accommodation was created at Horsham the troops used to erect their tents on Horsham Common. With the increase of enemy threats a

One of the Horsham depot armoury buildings, dating from 1804. (*Gote House*)

Barrack Cottage at Bishopstone, near Seaford, dates from the 1800s. It has been extensively modified over the years. (*Gote House*)

Barrack Cottages at Partridge Green. The name endorses the associations shown on maps of the area. (*Gote House*)

Barracks Office was established at Whitehall in London. Officers drew up plans for a sequence of twenty-three pre-fabricated wooden barrack-blocks to be sited across Sussex, to act as the front line of resistance between London and the coast.

Horsham barracks took 300 men some six weeks to build, at a cost estimated at £60,000. The timber-clad barracks and supporting buildings would have been built off-site and re-erected wherever they were deployed. The site of Horsham barracks now lies beneath residential property beside Worthing Road and Horsham Cricket Club. Barrack Field lay immediately outside the barracks and was used for training purposes. The buildings had brick foundations, with walls made of 12-in-wide planking. Roofing was scorched, using hot tar, to safeguard surfaces and the walls were treated with preservative. Troops lived in eight barrack-blocks, each of two storeys, with the upper rooms being open to the rafters. Soldiers slept in two-tier bunks and each floor could take 60 men. Some 960 troops could be accommodated in the barracks.

Officers had their own facilities at one end of the central parade ground. Service units, stables, cook-houses, a bakery and infirmary, mortuary, magazine and a guard-house made up the self-contained community.

It may be noted that Horsham barracks were typical of the army installations of the period located across the country. Place-names often offer a clue to military usage during the Napoleonic period of unrest.

THE ROYAL OXFORDSHIRE MILITIA MUTINY AT SEAFORD

With defence demands dominating local priorities Seaford bailiff Thomas Harben helped raise a militia force to combat the French threat. Harben adopted the role of captain of the two companies of Seaford Volunteers and in 1795 led the ending of the Royal Oxfordshire Militia mutiny from Blatchington barracks.

Although Blatchington is now absorbed into urban Seaford it was once a parish in its own right, stretching from The Salts wasteland to the west of Hawth valley. In 1794

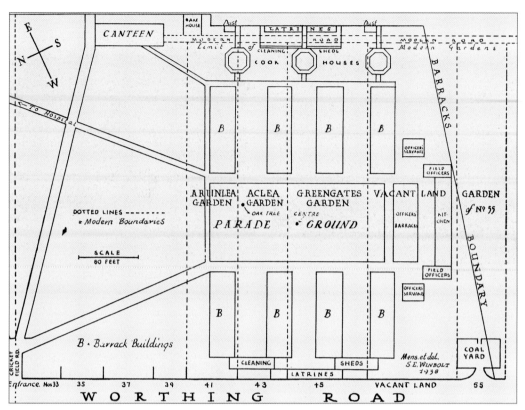

The southern half of Horsham barracks (1796–1815), superimposed on residential gardens in 1938. (*T.R. Beckett Ltd*)

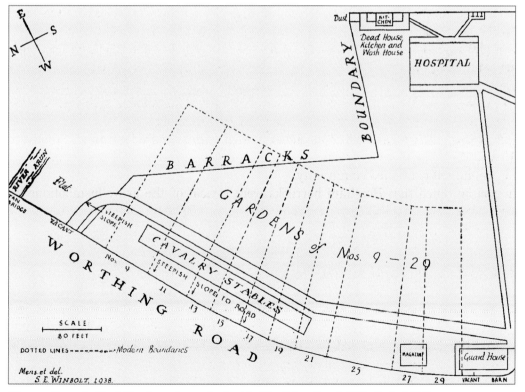

The northern half of Horsham barracks beside Worthing Road. (*T.R. Beckett Ltd*)

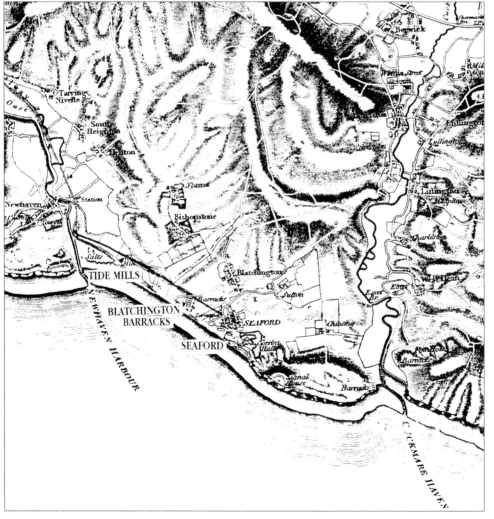

Privates Edward Cooke from Witney and Henry Parish of Chipping Norton were sentenced to die as scapegoats for the Seaford mutiny. They were executed by a firing squad made up of fellow Royal Oxfordshire Militia at Goldstone Bottom, Hove, on Saturday 13 June 1795. (*Royal Pavilion, Libraries & Museums, Brighton and Hove*)

The exposed position of Blatchington barracks can be seen on The Salts between Bishopstone Tide Mills and urban Seaford in this adapted 1873 map. (*Gote House*)

Blatchington Down was the location of extensive barracks, with a ten-gun battery. Construction of the barracks was rather slow and troops had to endure tented conditions. One gusty night the wind swept away the tents, kit and supplies of the resident Wiltshire Militia. The next incumbents were the Somerset and Oxford Militia who found that despite hutted facilities they still lacked a hospital, cook-house and decent roads. From their meagre pay of sixpence daily, plus fourpence for food, they had to go out into the local community and find their own food supplies. Unscrupulous businessmen profited vastly from the troops by supplying inferior foodstuffs often at inflated prices.

BACKGROUND TO THE MUTINY

The contrasting circumstances of officers and men could hardly have been more blatant than they were at the turn of the nineteenth century. Gentlemen officers enjoyed a flamboyant and fashionable lifestyle centred on London and regal Brighton, where troops had to march off daily for their principal training. After a harsh day's training and the march back to Blatchington, the troops were invariably exhausted and exasperated. Their modest food sources made them weak and ill, as many local traders exploited the very men who had taken up arms to defend the county. On Friday 17 April some 500 troops of the Royal Oxfordshire Militia fixed bayonets and marched on Seaford High Street, seizing all the available foodstuffs with the intention of selling off the goods to their comrades at token prices.

Captain Harben of the Seaford Volunteers, vastly outnumbered, pleaded with the Oxfords to abandon their cause and offered to buy back the food and then return it to troops at lower prices. The more boisterous rebels jeered at the Seaford Volunteers, although many relented and returned to their bleak quarters. The main rebellion force marched across to Bishopstone Tide Mills and stole 200 sacks of grain from a farm, loading the grain on to waggons; then they commandeered the sloop *Lucy* to go to Newhaven bridge and deposit the goods in a warehouse. A guard of sixty men remained at Newhaven, as the majority of the rebels went back to barracks at nightfall, after virtually taking over Newhaven port and selling parts of their hoard.

At dawn Captain Harben took control of the rebellion from Newhaven battery. Enlisted men with a pair of field guns quelled the rebels who had celebrated the previous night. Twenty-five rebels were force-marched to the House of Correction in Lewes, while the rest were sent back to Blatchington. Two days later the Lord Lieutenant of Sussex, the Duke of Richmond, was in the chair before the Lewes prisoners. At their subsequent courts martial four men received pardons and one, named John Haddocks, was sent to Botany Bay for ten years. Two profiteering privates, James Sykes and William Sampson, were hanged at Horsham gaol in June and six men were sentenced to receive up to 1,500 lashes. This cruel punishment was abandoned after the first trio had received 300 lashes.

On Saturday 13 June 1795 a crowd gathered at Goldstone Bottom in Hove (later the FA football ground) to witness the public execution of Privates Edward Cooke and Henry Parish. Scapegoats for the mutiny, they died bravely, kneeling at their coffins. The Oxford Militia had previously rebelled at Chichester and some were jailed after plundering a bakery. Their 'Royal' title was stripped from the regiment.

Calls for army reforms resounded across Britain, influenced by actions in France. The noted author William Cobbett and the radical Thomas Paine were among the idealist leaders of the period who led artisans with their apocalyptic theories.

LANGLEY POINT FORTS AND MARTELLO TOWERS

At the turn of the millennium it was deemed worthwhile to note the condition of certain coastal defences as they had been at the turn of the previous century. The following report from the Committee on Coast Defences, dated 17 January 1873, puts matters officially into context.

The Committee are of the opinion that abandonment of the [Martello] towers, when their protection against the sea began to become so costly, was a wise step; and they recommend that the same course be pursued in future. [They had been built between 1804 and 1814.]

Tower 72 near the Crumble Sluice was abandoned in 1850 and tower 71 in 1861. Nos 69 and 70 are washed by the sea at high water and their foundations are undermined. As the cost of protecting them would be inordinate the Committee recommend that they should be dismantled and disposed of as soon as their position becomes actually dangerous.

Langley Fort [note the 1873 spelling Langley – on the 1910 Ordnance Survey map the name is given as Langney] lies between Towers 66 [extant] and 67. A similar battery formerly existed between Towers 69 and 70. Both forts were originally constructed in 1759. The present fort was remodelled in 1855 as it now stands. It is of low command and though well situated for defending the coast, shingle has accumulated to such an extent in front of it that the shallow water near the shore is hidden from view, though seen by adjacent towers.

The enceinte consists of a scarp 10 feet high in front and a thin loop-holed wall 12 feet high in the rear, with a small two-storied defensible barracks on each flank affording accommodation for two officers and 50 men. Two ten-inch SB guns and four 32-pounder SB guns, all en barbette, close together and without traverses, compose the armament. The magazine for 300 barrels is very badly protected against fire. There is a tank for 3,180 gallons, but no casemated accommodation of any kind.

The rearmament of this work, with three or four efficient rifled guns well traversed and provision of adequate protection for its magazine is indispensable to render it of any value in an offensive point of view. The adjacent towers can afford a collateral defence, which would be very efficient if their masonry was protected in the manner already suggested.

As regards encroachment to the sea, Tower 67 will probably be safe for 80 years hence, the fort for above one hundred years and Tower 66 for an indefinitely greater time. [Elsewhere Tower 67 is recorded as being destroyed by Royal Artillery practice in 1870, along with No. 68 on St Anthony's Hill. Nos 69 and 70 were lost to the sea round 1872.]

Tower No. 68 occupies a small conical hill a mile from the shore – well situated to command communication from the Crumble Beach to the interior, at the junction of the Bourne and Pevensey Levels. It has a ditch and forms an excellent nucleus of field works on Anthony Hill and at Langley Farm.

So ends the report of the Committee on Coast Defences, dated 17 January 1873. There is some variation on the fate of certain Martello Towers from previously published accounts.

The westerly profile of the long-
gone 1855 Langley Fort, recorded
in 1893. (*Public Record Office*)

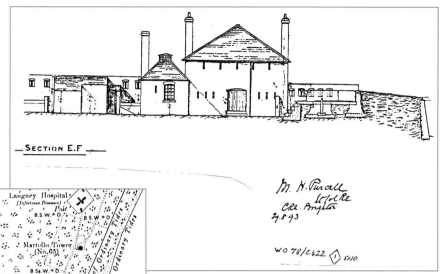

Langley Fort, on the coast at the Crumbles,
Eastbourne, is outlined on this 1910 map. However,
on the 1938 revised map only the inland outline
appears. Tower 66 remains in robust form west of
the new Marina entry. (*Gote House*)

High tides and sea defence work near the
Eastbourne Marina in the winter of 2000 revealed
a mixture of Napoleonic and 1940s defence works.
(*Gote House*)

Still surviving on the shore are Tower 66 at the Marina estuary and Tower 64 to the east. The Ordnance Survey map of 1910 shows the outline of the 1850s Langley Fort mid-way between Towers 65 and 66 where the 1794 East Fort was sited, with the fort embracing the high water mark of ordinary tides. The 1925 map revision, with 1938 additions, shows only the inland small defensible barracks on each flank east of Tower 66. Thus all the information to hand suggests that the Langley Fort of the 1850s was eclipsed by the ravages of tide and circumstance.

ROUSSILLON BARRACKS, CHICHESTER

The name Roussillon commemorates the Royal Sussex Regiment which took part in the defeat of the French Roussillon Regiment at the time of the capture of Quebec. The barracks in Broyle Road, Chichester, were built in 1803 to accommodate 1,500 officers and men. A few years later the complex housed Peninsular War prisoners. The barracks' long association with the Royal Sussex Regiment commenced in about 1808.

Between 1939 and 1945 Depot Rear Details remained at the camp and it was also occupied by 45 ITC 70th Young Soldiers and the United States Army. In the mid-1960s the barracks were extensively rebuilt and then reopened for the Royal Military Police, who have since then occupied the complex as their training and administration centre.

Colourful stained-glass windows in the depot chapel depict Royal Military Police personnel in action. (*Courtesy of the Royal Military Police Training School*)

Stages of barrack
accommodation at
Chichester. Top: the original
elegant castellated
accommodation built for
troops in 1803. Middle:
Sandhurst barracks in
Whistler Avenue are typical
of mid-twentieth-century
barracks architecture.
Lower: Modern estate life is
represented by the married
quarters block at Roussillon
Barracks. (*All pictures by
courtesy of the Royal
Military Police Training
School*)

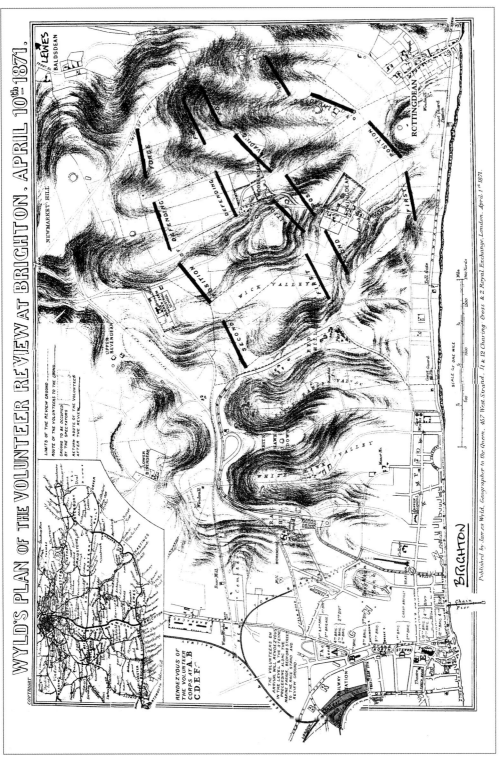

Colourful parades and exercises were commonplace around Brighton in the eighteenth and nineteenth centuries. James Wyld's official plan shows the Volunteer Review of 10 April 1871, a time when local brigades played a vital role in Britain's armed forces. The Volunteers assembled between The Level to the Steyne in Brighton, and marched along Marine Parade and Bedford Street up to the racecourse, before proceeding to the downland Review Ground around Ovingdean. (*Adapted from Brighton Reference Library*)

The A27 Lewes Road frontage of Brighton barracks is seen here in the late 1980s, before the down-sizing of the establishment and the demolition of this and many other buildings at the 17-acre site. (*Christopher Horlock*)

BRIGHTON BARRACKS

Brighton was seen as a prime target for invading forces because it gave direct access to London through the natural gap of the South Downs. Like other coastal communities, Brighton featured a variety of batteries and defence works up to the turn of the eighteenth century. In the late nineteenth century a series of annual camps were staged on the downland around Brighton and these soon became a national spectacle as people came to watch the manoeuvres, entranced by the gaiety and colour of troop movements. Many thousands of troops were engaged in training exercises and mock battles. Preston cavalry barracks rose to prominence as the town expanded. The original timber-clad buildings from 1794 – initially designed to house 170 privates and NCOs, together with stables for 215 horses – were gradually replaced by more substantial accommodation. Workshops were also constructed at the barracks in an attractive yellow-brick pattern.

The first barracks were built in a remote valley a mile inland from the coast and were named after the hamlet of Preston, which is a few miles west of Brighton over Hollingdean Hill, astride the A23 London Road. The name Preston barracks was superceded by the more appropriate Brighton barracks as urban growth rapidly encompassed the walled military establishment. Phased barracks expansion took place during the Boer War and the two twentieth-century world wars witnessed extensive utilisation of Brighton barracks.

In May 1999 government policy decreed the phased demise of the site. A Royal Military Police company and a Territorial Army unit that had been based at the Lewes Road barracks since 1982 were to close that month, despite concern that the TA was being wound down at the time of the Balkans dispute. The majority of the 17-acre Brighton barracks site had been sold off during the 1980s to form the Pavilion Centre retail park. The final 5 acres were to be sold off in mid-1999 – the once proud military tradition being perpetuated in a minor way by the inclusion of an Army Cadets training facility.

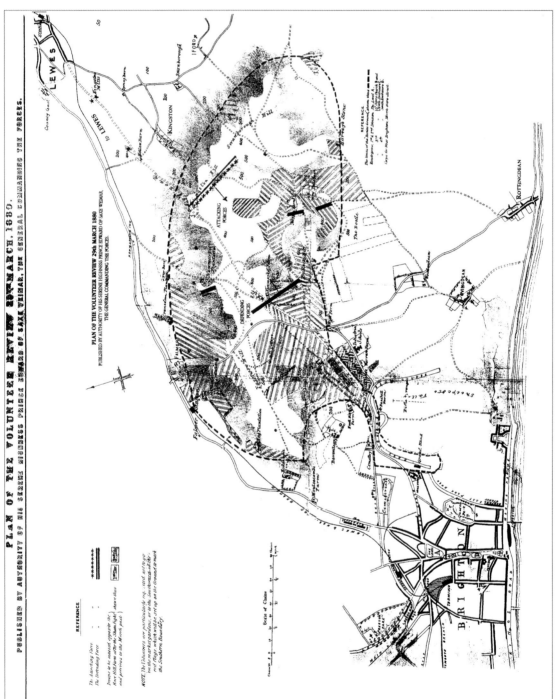

Up to 20,000 troops would be engaged in the sequence of exercises and parades centred on Brighton in the latter nineteenth century. Special trains and camps were prepared and an influx of soldiers' families, merchants and camp follcwers flooded into the town for the annual Easter exercises. On 29 March 1880 mock battles took place on the rolling pastures around Bullock Hill and Kingston village between Brighton and Lewes. (*Adapted from Brighton Reference Library*)

2

The First World War

A CALL TO ARMS!

4th (Home Service) BATTALION
ROYAL SUSSEX REGIMENT.

This Regiment is now being raised at Horsham to form a Reserve to the 4th Battalion Royal Sussex Regiment, which has been accepted for Foreign Service. A recruit (subject to the conditions stated below) can decide whether he will enlist for Foreign or Home Service.

CONDITIONS.

TERM.—Duration of the War, or not exceeding 4 years.

AGE.—(a) Foreign Service, 19-35 } Height 5ft. 2in.; Chest 33in.
(b) Home Service, 17-35 }
Ex-Sergeants up to age of 50 years; Ex-Corporals up to age of 45 years.

PAY.—7s. per week (exclusive of board and lodging).

ALLOWANCES (for upkeep of Kit).—1s. 2d. per week.

SEPARATION ALLOWANCES.

Wife, 9s. a week.	Wife and 4 children, 16s. 9d. per week.
Wife and 1 child, 10s. 11d. per week.	Each additional child, 2s. per week.
Wife and 2 children, 12s. 10d. „	Each Motherless child, 3s. per week.
Wife and 3 children, 14s. 9d. „	A child means a boy up to 14 years and a girl up to 16 years.

Enlist at once—delay is dangerous. Apply at nearest Police Station or at THE DEPOT, THE DRILL HALL, HORSHAM.

Hon. Recruiting Officer for this District
Who will enlist men and give all information :

J. A. MINCHIN, Esq.
"WANTLEY," HENFIELD.

HORSHAM. OCT.ᵉ 1914.

As the enormous demands of war were contemplated reservist units were recruited. This daunting poster from 1914 attempts to lure men into uniform. (*Gote House*)

The Royal Sussex Regiment in action at the Battle of Loos, 1915. Sergeant Harry Wells of the 2nd Battalion is depicted leading troops forward in this oil painting by Ernest Ibbetson. Sergeant Wells won a posthumous Victoria Cross for his bravery in this action. (*Gardiner Graphics*)

During the First World War the Sussex countryside resonated with the sounds of troops in training. On sloping woodlands at Forest Row a vast army camp was created. Today a modest memorial details the actions of the men from all over the Empire who trained on terrain now used as a golf course. (*Gote House*)

European unrest in mid-1914 escalated rapidly. While suffragettes sought emancipation in Britain a European arms race fuelled fears of war. First Lord of the Admiralty Winston Churchill demanded £2.5 million for the Royal Navy to boost oil stocks and expedite battleship and aircraft construction. He declared: 'It is our intention to put eight squadrons into service in the time it takes Germany to build five.' The government was also heavily occupied with unrest in Ireland. On 28 June Archduke Franz Ferdinand, the heir to the Austro-Hungarian Empire, and his wife were assassinated, and then on 23 July Austria made war inevitable with a series of demands on neighbouring Serbia. A week later British attempts to mediate in the growing crisis in Europe were rejected by the Kaiser as insolent. Austrians supporting the Kaiser's stance declared war. Britain waited, fearing the worst, and war against Germany was declared on 4 August. Throughout Britain, people went about cheering and singing the national anthem.

The British Expeditionary Force of 70,000 men secretly crossed the Channel and fought alongside French and Belgian troops in the tense battle for the town of Mons. On 23 August they began to retreat and British forces sustained their first heavy losses.

THE ENIGMATIC VOICE OF PROTEST

Of all the facets of the First World War it is the voice of protest, especially of the war poets, that is perhaps the most intriguing.

The gung-ho 'it will all be over by Christmas' call of the nation's recruiting crowds and the hype of the so-called Pals Brigades had dragged the warring nations towards a defensive stalemate. At the horrendous Battle of the Somme some 57,470 men were killed or wounded on the first day, 1 July 1916. Winston Churchill wrote that 'Generals were content to fight machine-gun bullets with the breasts of gallant men.' The 1917 Battle of Passchendaele saw trench warfare at its worst, with heavy rain and sucking mud and more horrific losses. The catalogue of futile campaigns continued month after month.

Among the growing number of protesters complaining about armchair patriots and lush lifestyles at Army headquarters, about inaccurate press reports, about profiteers and the hypocrisy of war were the war poets. Prominent among them was Siegfried Sassoon. Born into a privileged family in Brenchley, Kent, he could have paid for a lighter appointment than serving on the Western Front. On 3 August 1914 he enlisted in the Sussex Yeomanry, after sleeping for three days on the floor of the enlisting office at Tunbridge Wells. In May 1915 he took a commission in the Royal Welch Fusiliers and in late November 1915 joined their 1st Battalion in France. In June 1916 he was awarded the Military Cross for gallantry in action, before being invalided home with trench fever. In mid-February 1916 he was back at the infantry base at Rouen, only to be wounded in the shoulder the next month. In May and June 1917 he was in a convalescent home at Chapelwood Manor, Nutley, Sussex.

In July 1917 Sassoon was diagnosed with shellshock and sent to the experimental Craiglockhart War Hospital near Edinburgh, where he influenced another noted poet Wilfred Owen. On 30 July 1917 Sassoon's controversial statement against the continuation of the war was read out in Parliament and reported in *The Times*. In 1918 he was back in service in Egypt and Palestine, then in France where on 13 July he was wounded in the head. He retired from the Army on 12 March 1919. He continued to write books and poems until his death in 1967.

'THE GENERAL'

Siegfried Sassoon

'Good morning; good morning!' the
    General said
When we met him last week on our way
    to the line.
Now the soldiers he smiled at are most of
    'em dead.
And we're cursing his staff for
    incompetent swine.
'He's a cheery old card,' grunted Harry to
    Jack
As they slogged up to Arras with rifle and
    pack.

But he did for them both by his plan of
    attack.

'BLIGHTERS'

Siegfried Sassoon

The house is crammed: tier beyond tier they
    grin
And cackle at the Show, while prancing
    ranks
Of harlots shrill the chorus, drunk with din;
'We're sure the Kaiser loves our dear old
    Tanks!'

I'd like to see a Tank come down the stalls,
Lurching to rag-time tunes, or 'Home sweet
    Home',
And there'd be no more jokes in Music-halls
To mock the riddled corpses round
    Bapaume.

In 1914 22-year-old Second-Lieutenant Vincent Waterfall, of 5 Squadron RFC, became the first British pilot to die in action when his Avro 504 biplane, no. 390, was brought down by infantry fire over enemy terrain. The incident also claimed the life of his observer, Lieutenant Charles G.C. Bayly. Both men are buried in the Tournai Communal Cemetery Allied Extension.

The two men took off on a reconnaissance flight on 22 August 1914 and were reported missing the following day. It was the first time that an aircraft had failed to return from flights over enemy-held territory, and sadly it served to warn German intelligence of the Allied presence. The observer's report, part completed, was found by Belgian peasants close to the wreckage and eventually made its way to the War Office in London.

Vincent Waterfall's parents are buried in the grounds of St John's Church at Burgess Hill, and the gravestone in the centre includes a commemorative inscription to their son. (*Geoff Bridger*)

In July 2001 the Royal Sussex Regiment celebrated the 300th anniversary of its foundation in Belfast in 1701 as the 35th Foot. Members of the Regimental Association enjoyed a luncheon gathering and a Beating the Retreat ceremony at Christs Hospital School in Horsham. Six Victoria Crosses won by members of the regiment were on display, as well as a magnificent set of silver drums presented to the regiment by the people of Sussex. On 31 December 1966 the Royal Sussex Regiment was amalgamated with other regiments to form the Queens' Regiment and in 1992 it became part of the Princess of Wales' Royal Regiment. (*Gote House*)

Many of the Royal Sussex Regiment archives are maintained on public display at the seafront Redoubt Fortress Museum in Eastbourne. In 1800 the regiment played a leading role in the capture of Malta and its Kings Colour was the first British flag to be hoisted on the ramparts after the island was captured. The regiment served in India during its development and helped to quell the infamous Indian Mutiny of 1857. Strong ties were formed with the 107th (Bengal Infantry) Regiment. In 1881 the 35th Foot and the 107th Bengal Regiments formed the 1st and 2nd Battalions of the Royal Sussex Regiment. During the First World War the Royal Sussex formed 23 battalions, and lost some 6,800 men in battle. The enemy nicknamed the Royal Sussex Regiment 'The Iron Regiment'. The regiment took part in some of the most famous battles of the twentieth century, including Gallipoli, the Somme, Passchendaele and later Monte Cassino, El Alamein and the Burma campaign. (*Gote House*)

AIRCRAFT MANUFACTURE AT MIDDLETON-ON-SEA

The White and Thompson aircraft plant, a few miles east of Bognor at Middleton-on-Sea, was created on a 7½-acre greenfield site purchased in 1910. The founders – Norman Thompson, an electrical engineer, and the wealthy Dr Douglas White – intended to promote experimental work on aero techniques and on aircraft production. The site was chosen for its proximity to a broad area of compact, well-drained sand (at low tide) that made it eminently suitable as a landing ground. Workshops and offices were established some 25 yards above the high water level and a slipway was laid to the sands.

White and Thompson's No. 1 biplane appeared in 1911. Its ash frame fuselage, clad in light steel panels, was built by the Daimler Car Company in Coventry, and it had an elaborate undercarriage comprising four castoring wheels with pneumatic tyres. It had elevators fitted at the rear fuselage and a sail-type rudder with elevators mounted on the nose. The wings were clad with 23swg aluminium. It was powered by two rotary Gnome Rhône engines, placed side-by-side, and cross-belted in case one engine failed.

Automobile engineer F.W. Lanchester had been engaged as a design consultant, but after abortive trials of experimental aircraft he left the company. One early biplane was called *Grey Angel* and trials commenced in 1910. The experience of production techniques was undoubtedly of value to the young firm, but *Grey Angel* never left the ground and was scrapped in 1911. When Lanchester left the firm Norman Thompson built a plane to his own design. The prototype flew successfully for some time, until it crashed on the rocks on the Middleton coast in 1914.

In 1913 Norman Thompson secured agency rights for marketing Curtiss flying-boats in Britain and the Dominions, and thought it appropriate to develop the Middleton aerodrome with larger buildings and a flying school. With the outbreak of the First World War the company undertook the design and manufacture of flying-boats for military use. The enterprising firm actually built around 300 aircraft, including a number under contract for Short Bros and the Franco-British Aviation Company.

Despite a flurry of success the firm was constantly under financial pressure. Government influence led it to undertake new buildings, but then the orders for aircraft failed to materialise. Allegedly dubious dealings with Curtiss added to their problems. It is said that Norman Thompson never forgave either the British government or Curtiss for their roles in these dealings, which effectively ended his dream of manufacturing civilian aircraft successfully. At the close of 1918 official receivers were appointed and Norman Thompson settled in France – insisting in his will that he should not be buried in England or the USA.

Handley-Page Ltd acquired the Norman Thompson Flight Company's assets in 1919, intending to start passenger flights from the coast. Flying-boats were adapted for this project at Middleton, although the plan came to naught. In February 1920 the airfield site was auctioned and was bought by Sir Walter Aston Blunt.

One large hangar was sold to Bognor Council, which re-erected it at Waterloo Square as the Winter Gardens pavilion. It thrived as a theatre and dance hall, until it was demolished following a catastrophic fire in 1948. The Norman-Thompson aircraft factory site, with a few of the original buildings left, opened in 1922 as the New City Holiday Camp. It was always overshadowed by the nearby Butlins Holiday Camp. In 1997 the site was sold to Crest Homes, and the old aero sheds were demolished to make way for the modern Saxon Reach residential estate. The street names Norman Way and Thompson Road are the only clues to the former coastal aircraft manufacture site.

The innovative Bognor Bloater biplane was constructed by the Norman Thompson Flight Company in 1915. The frail aircraft featured a fuselage made by securing plywood panels by means of copper wire, which resembled fish scales and is how it acquired its name. (*H.J.F. Thompson*)

Towards the end of the First World War an agreement with the American Air Force led to work starting on an airfield at Rustington. It was never finished and in 1922 the hangars were relocated as warehouses besides the Arun river. (*H.J.F. Thompson*)

The sheer size of the army camps can be gauged by this view entitled Brigade Road. It is believed to show South Camp, Seaford, which was sited between Chyngton Road and the main road into the town. (*Patricia Berry*)

In some districts local people can point out structural artefacts from the old army camps, especially where hutting has been adapted for private dwellings. A more dramatic sign of a military presence is this former training ground near Seaford. (*Gote House*)

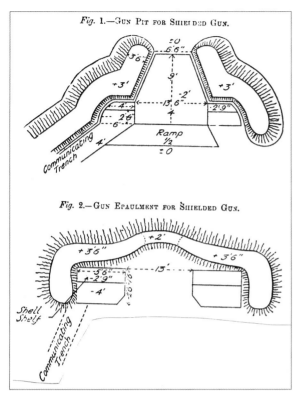

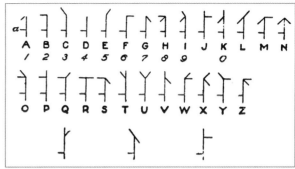

Semaphore alphabet, numerals and special signs as detailed in a field-service pocket book issued by General Staff, the War Office, London, 1914. (*War Office*)

The First World War dragged the Allies into mechanised conflict, transforming centuries of military techniques. Traditional field procedures, like those seen here, had to be revised for modern warfare. (*War Office*)

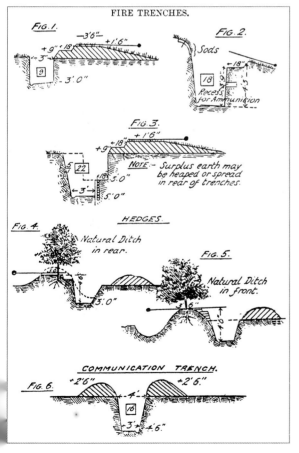

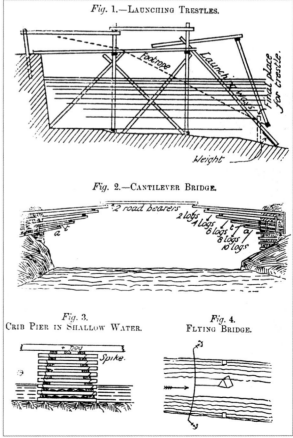

Members of the Old Aschamian
Society gratefully record that on
this ground there thrived
Ascham St Vincents
Preparatory School
from 1889 to 1939
and
Ascham the College
Preparatory School
from 1946 to 1977.
'Virtue et Valore.'

In memory of 49 gallant men
who were at school here in
their early boyhood and gave
their lives 1914–1918 in
the Great War.

Institutional colleges and convalescent homes were a feature of many Sussex towns. Many proliferate to this day, but a greater number have moved inland or ceased to function. One striking memorial from the First World War is this brick and stone arch, a relic of the former Ascham St Vincents Preparatory School in Carlisle Road, Eastbourne. The Ascham educational premises have long gone and the grounds have been built over by modern homes. The college archway is intact, however, and is inscribed in memory of former pupils who gave their lives during the First World War. (*Gote House*)

German U-boat patrols became a deadly phenomenon during the First World War. In August 2001 a diving team from Tunbridge Wells British Sub-Aqua Club recovered a rare U-boat gun from the English Channel off Newhaven. The 16-ft-long, 2-tonne weapon from UB *130* was said to be in amazing condition, although it had been under the sea for some eighty years. The gun is now displayed outside Newhaven Local & Maritime Museum. On 15 April 1919 UB *121* and UB *130* were being towed to Cherbourg as part of the German war reparations to France. The hawser broke and UB *130* sank 8 miles off Eastbourne. UB *121*, however, drifted ashore, settling at Birling Gap where her bow jammed into the remains of the tramp ship *Ushla*, which had become stranded on the shore under Bailey's Brow west of Birling Gap in November 1916. *Ushla* remained below the Seven Sisters cliffs until 1928 when a firm of Welsh iron smelters actioned salvage rights to the wreck, laying a narrow-gauge industrial rail track over the rocks to recover valuable metals. The 290-tonne UB class were small in size at 92 ft long. The prefabricated vessels were built up at coastal ports and featured a pair of 18-in torpedo tubes. They were particularly used in shallow seas like the English Channel. The 3.4-in gun was forward of the conning tower. The even smaller UC types carried neither guns or torpedos, but were instead fitted with six mine carriers making up twelve mines. These vessels also patrolled mainly in shallow waters. (*Gote House*)

Among the exhibits at Filching Manor, Jevington, is this 1906 Armstrong-Whitworth gun from the Tribal class destroyer HMS *Gurkha*, which sank off Beachy Head on 8 February 1917 after striking a mine; 87 sailors lost their lives. (*Gote House*)

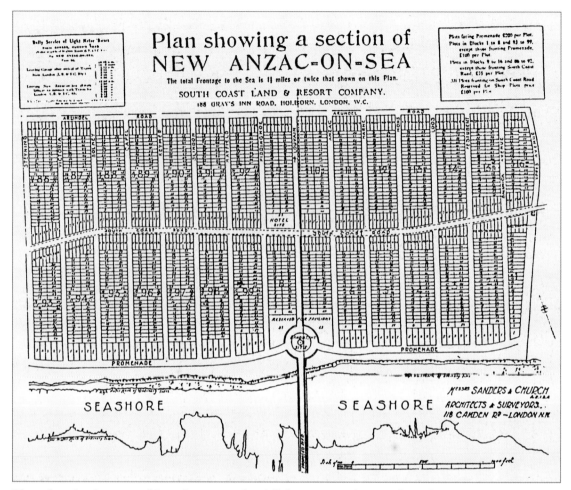

The urban development of Peacehaven, on the cliffs between Brighton and Newhaven, emerged after the First World War from the enterprising Charles Neville's vision of a garden-city-by-the-sea. Ranch-style timber homes sprang up spasmodically and earned the area its 'shanty town' tag, but Peacehaven did offer homes and employment to returning soldiers. Much of the building material came from salvage at redundant army camps in Seaford.

This 1916 Peacehaven Estate Company plan shows avenues initially named after infamous battlefields: Louvain (now Southview), Marne (Vernon), Loos (Seaview), Festubert (Friars), Salonica (Cornwall) and Ypres (Searle). A recreation area was titled Anzac Park before the Ministry of Agriculture requisitioned the land for food production. At one stage it was proposed to call the community New-Anzac-on-Sea in memory of the Australian and New Zealand troops committed to the Gallipoli peninsula, after a ballot of titles. When it was later considered that the Gallipoli association was too hallowed to be linked with the rambling urban environs the name Lureland appeared, but in February 1917 the title Peacehaven was adopted to help sell the idea of living atop the bleak windy cliffs.

Peacehaven's network of avenues soon absorbed the former Telscombe Cliffs pastures where a 50-acre landing ground was created in 1917 to protect Channel shipping. It was manned by the 6th Brigade Home Defence. No. 78 Squadron was formed here, with neighbouring flights in support. A change in enemy plans made the airfield redundant and after nine months the squadron moved to Essex. There were no permanent buildings, canvas hangars and tents serving all needs initially.

Later U-boat attacks in the Channel led to the construction of two hangars, Armstrong sheds and a guard-room/diner with a service road. When the occupying 514 Flight of No. 242 Squadron was disbanded in late 1919 the landing ground was converted into a rehabilitation centre for wounded ex-officers. Most of the buildings were demolished or removed but a pair of air station buildings survived to the 1950s when the land was absorbed into expanding Peacehaven. (*Gote House*)

Ticehurst, 2½ miles east of Wadhurst, is rich in rural charm. In the vestibule of St Mary's Church is a Roll of Honour to 331 Ticehurst men and women who served in the First World War. The majority of them were in C Company of the 5th (Cinque Ports) Battalion of the Royal Sussex Regiment under the command of Captain George Courthope of Whiligh. (*Gote House*)

Sixty-two Ticehurst soldiers did not return. Most of them perished in mid-May 1915 when the Royal Sussex Regiment (Cinque Ports) was cut to pieces on Aubers Ridge during the battle of Festuburt. Eleven of the casualties were employed by Coopers Stores and their names are recorded on a brass plaque on the wall of the shop premises (formerly Coopers) near St Mary's Church. The pentice roof of the shop is supported by cast-iron columns – a proud reminder of local industry and times past in the district. The 'lucky villages' of Sussex were so-called after communities that escaped the loss of men in the epic First World War battles. The notorious 'Pals Brigades' policy tragically accounted for the swift demise of large groups of men from particular communities in enemy action. (*Gote House*)

The village war memorial at Ditchling, under Ditchling Beacon near Lewes, photographed after Remembrance Sunday, 2000. The monument commemorates armed services personnel from various theatres of war. (*Gote House*)

Ditchling is renowned as an artists' retreat, and prominent in the colony from 1907 to 1924 was the influential sculptor, engraver and letter-cutter Eric Gill (left). He was born into a large Brighton family dominated by his church minister father with his idealistic religious ethics and soldiering ideals. Tales of the Boer War and stirring First World War patriotism led Eric to dismiss wars as jingoistic imperialism.

As a young man Eric enlisted in the Queen's Westminster Rifle Corps. Called up in July 1915, he found himself, aged 32 years, engaged in army exercises at Lewes racecourse. He contested his need to serve and enlisted instead in the Home Defence Brigade at Burgess Hill. Called up again in late 1918, he was sent to Blandford Forum as an RAF driver.

In the 1930s his ideals encompassed pacifism, and perhaps his greatest work *Creation* was commissioned during his all-art-is-propaganda period. His engraving was the British government's gift to the League of Nations Organisation at their headquarters building in Geneva. It was made of three panels, each of seventeen sections. The centre panel was 20 ft long and 7 ft tall. Eric Gill's most enduring legacy, however, is his innovative **GILL SANS** typeface. Gill's nephew John Skelton (1923–99) lived in Sussex all his life. A renowned artist and engraver, he cut the memorial stones for Winston Churchill and Viscount Montgomery. (*Gote House*)

In 1917 a RNAS seaplane base was created on sheltered shingle between Newhaven harbour's eastern arm and the redundant Tide Mills site. Activity at RNAS Newhaven, however, was short-lived and by 1920 the buildings were surplus to needs and staff and equipment were dispersed. (*Gote House*)

The costly timber hangars had but a short life at Newhaven and were sold off at auction. British Railways acquired one of the £500,000 hangars and re-erected it as a supplies store close to Wimbledon station – where it remains today, protected by its Listed status. (*Peter Fellows*)

This weather-beaten curio, standing atop a headland half a mile west of the landmark Devil's Dyke public house north of Brighton, has a link with the RFC. Generations of farmers have passed on its name as 'the bomb house'. The brick rectangular property has been the subject of lengthy investigation by members of the Sussex Industrial Archaeology Society. Originally it is thought that the roofless structure was conceived as a viewing gallery, or obscura, over the Wealden plains, before it was taken over as a bomb store for RFC airmen training nearby. Records of the installation do not exist in local authority offices or on maps.

Among a variety of amusements at the Devil's Dyke in about 1900 was an aerial cableway that crossed the depths of the famous gorge. The cableway, suspended between ugly towers, was erected in 1894 and traded until 1909, and is understood to have been extant during the First World War. Trainee airmen used the cableway to drop 50lb Cooper bombs into the valley; the bombs were triggered by a stop in the centre of the cable run. (*Gote House*)

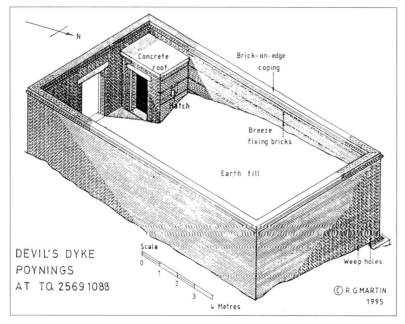

An excellent 1995 architectural drawing of the Devil's Dyke obscura, which became known as the 'bomb house' after utilisation by RFC trainees. Sadly such illustrations may in time be all that remain of the structure as the unkempt walls are becoming increasingly cracked. (*Plan by courtesy of Ron Martin*)

The Devil's Dyke aerial cableway took just 2 minutes to traverse the ravine. It functioned between October 1894 and 1909 and was later adopted by RFC airmen for bomb practice exercises. A 650-ft clear span was doubled, making up the total distance between the suspended catenary. At the midway point passengers were 230 ft above the ground. Cables were sometimes 'removed' from photographs and prints. The refreshment rooms, cable houses and golf club-house have long since been levelled. (*Gote House*)

The Devil's Dyke gorge. On the right is a concrete slab platform, the only surviving artefact of the aerial cableway. Less appreciative of the scenery was Sergeant W.F. Kenwood of the RCAF, based at Biggin Hill. His Spitfire W3120 of 92 Squadron crashed in the gorge on Sunday 1 August 1941 and burned out. Luckily the pilot escaped serious injury. (*Gote House*)

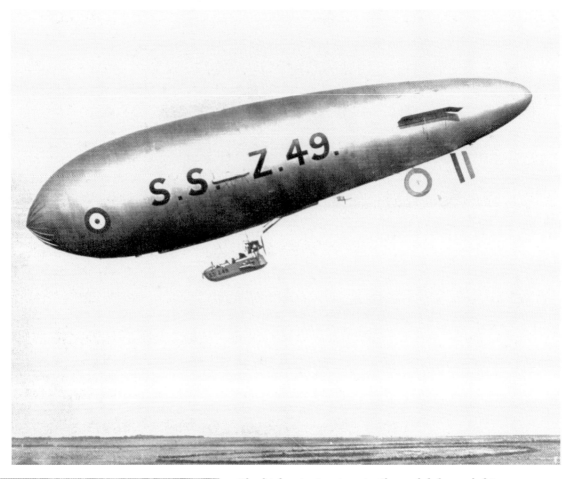

The high priority given to Channel defences led to numerous RFC aerodromes and RNAS stations being established along the south coast. Most successful of the RNAS airships was the Submarine Scout, powered by a 75hp Rolls-Royce Hawk engine. Seventy-six airships of this specification were built for patrol work, with some flights lasting for many gruelling hours. On 1 August 1918 Submarine Scout Z39, from RNAS Polegate, remained in flight for 50 hours and 55 minutes. (*Gote House*)

The rudimentary conditions for crew members can be gauged in this view of a German Zeppelin R-V that made its maiden flight in April 1915. Some of the R-series Giants had six engines; this R-V version had five engines located in the nacelles and nose. The maximum bomb-load was 2,000 lb. In one early R-type raid a 660lb bomb entered the basement of Odhams print works in London, resulting in 123 casualties.

In mid-August 2001 the name Zeppelin rose from the ashes of its predecessors. For the first time since the 1937 *Hindenburg* disaster passengers could book flights on a new Zeppelin NT. This airship is filled with the inert gas helium, rather than the highly inflammable hydrogen used in earlier examples. (*Gote House*)

Adastra Park is central to the pleasant Wealden village of Hassocks, which nestles under the outlook from the famous Jack and Jill windmills on Clayton Hill. Along with Stafford House, the popular leisure grounds were donated to the community by the locally prominent Stafford family in memory of their son Frederick John Ewart Stafford. He joined the RFC direct from Mill Hill School, and was shot down over Neuville Vitasse on 11 April 1917. His BE2e biplane, no. A2813 of 8 Squadron RFC, was wrecked. Although badly wounded he managed to land just inside our lines, on ground taken from the enemy only a few hours previously. Lieutenant G.E. Gibbons, his observer, escaped unwounded and managed to clamber to a shell-hole. He survived. Ewart Stafford was rescued some hours later, very weak from loss of blood, and later gangrene set in. His leg was amputated, but he died on 22 April in Abbeville base hospital. He was buried at Abbeville Communal Cemetery Extension, France. (*Gote House*)

The RFC motto *Per Ardua ad Astra* – Through Difficulties to the Stars – originated in 1912 and was adopted from the Irish Mulvany family, whose creed was quoted in H. Rider Haggard's book *The People of the Mist*.

The fledgling Royal Flying Corps of 1912 was commanded by 34-year-old Captain Frederick H. Sykes of the 15th (Kings) Hussars with a nominal force of just four aircraft. Captain Sykes soon sought ideas for a motto and J.S. Yule, a young Royal Engineers officer, suggested *Per Ardua ad Astra* as being appropriate for the embryonic national air force. On 11 December 1914 the RFC adopted the red, white and blue roundel as its identifier. The Union flag was thought too easily mistaken for the German cross. (*Gote House*)

Light industrial development around Willingdon Levels, Eastbourne, has virtually swallowed up the once flourishing St Anthony's aerodrome. The pioneering aero workshops and flying school, dating from 1911, have recently been the subject of comprehensive research by members of Eastbourne Local History Society. The results have been published as *A History of the Eastbourne Aviation Company*. One artefact from that period is the air station guard-house which survives in Leeds Avenue. (*Gote House*)

ST ANTHONY'S AERODROME

With the outbreak of the First World War on 4 August 1914, the Eastbourne Aircraft Company's aerodrome, hangars and workshops were taken over by the Admiralty. By 1917 RNAS St Anthony's had another fifteen wood and canvas Bessoneau hangars, each housing six aircraft. Pilots navigated the numerous drainage ditches across the meadows by ramps and bridges. There was also a seaplane factory, consisting of a large hangar on Pevensey Road, with a turntable and rail track down to high tide levels.

Little remains of the 50-acre St Anthony's airfield which hosted a flying school and assembly sheds for BE2c aircraft for the RNAS and later 150 Avro 504A and 504Ks for the RFC. Industrial areas, wider roads and housing now dominate the land around Lottbridge Drove, which once bordered the airfield. However, on Willingdon Levels the airfield can still be appreciated. A hangar base remains off Leeds Avenue, the hangar itself having finally been felled by the 1987 storms. When the occupant of the former guard-house (above) moved in over fifty years ago it still had its corrugated iron roof and steel bars across smaller windows. It is now called The Bungalow. Leeds Avenue, it is said, took its name from the city where many of the recruits came from.

Between 1919 and 1920 some 256 British airfields were closed. Four years later the RAF had only twenty-seven airfields and just seventeen civilian aerodromes existed. Gradually new military airfields were developed and others were upgraded as further threats of warfare in Europe rumbled on. Into the 1930s the continued growth of Nazi Germany influenced the expansion period of RAF progression. Between 1935 and the early 1940s a total of eighty-nine new airfields were established.

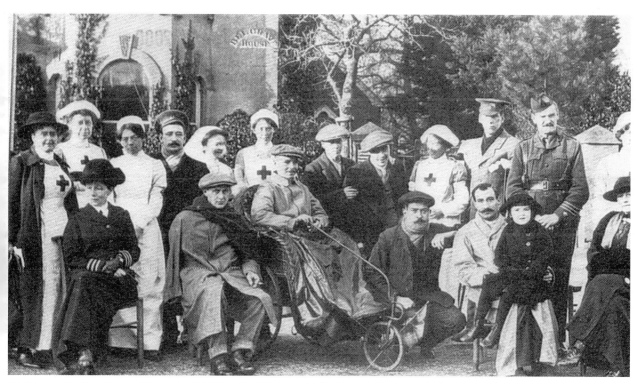

Littlehampton's Belgrave House in FitzAlan Road was one of the countless stately homes and institutions requisitioned as hospitals for Allied casualties in the First World War. (*H.J.F. Thompson*)

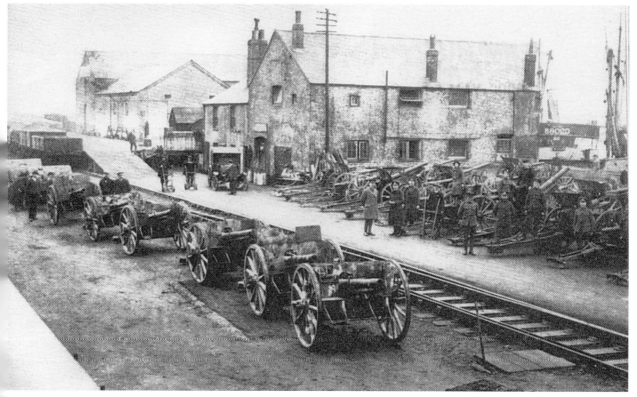

The prizes of war. These captured German field-guns are lined up on Littlehampton railway wharf in 1918. (*H.J.F. Thompson*)

This postcard was sent by a soldier based at Lydd Camp, Kent. Note the peculiar containers stacked to the left of the scene. The demand for horses stripped the nation's countryside of its equine pulling power to such an extent that farming never recovered. This factor hastened the widespread mechanisation of agricultural implements in the 1920s. (*Gote House*)

Family photographs of the time would invariably include some members in uniform. Here, the Army, RFC and Royal Navy are all represented. Standing is Harry Jenkins of Tunbridge Wells who enlisted in the RFC. At the front is his brother Ted of the Canadian 54th Kootenay Battalion. The Royal Navy is represented by their sister, proudly wearing her naval attire. Two of the ladies are wearing Woolwich Arsenal Munitions factory badges, where they worked. Ted had emigrated to Canada in about 1907 and together with thousands of other Canadians had joined the Army to fight the common enemy. (*Ted Awcock*)

3

The Second World War

This interesting view was taken from inside the South
Heighton tunnels of HMS *Forward* in early October 1941.
These western exit workings beside the A26
Beddingham–Newhaven road were concealed with
camouflaged netting. Royal Engineers of No. 2 Section 172
Tunnelling Company removed chalk spoil via the narrow
gauge rail track laid for the excavations. (*Imperial War
Museum H14501*)

Sixty years on, odd artefacts from the Second World War remain in a few places on the South Downs. A cluster of a dozen Home Guard slit trench gun positions still exists near the Beddingham Hill radio masts near Lewes. (*Gote House*)

The view down Beddingham Hill along the sweeping wartime metalled by-way, adopted as a tank road, towards Little Dene, the A27 and Glynde village. Tragically the hills here witnessed a number of Allied aircraft crashes. (*Gote House*)

Volunteer, Militia and Reservist forces have been utilised in various guises over the centuries. Initially, in 1939 volunteers and men with Reserved Occupation status were encouraged to join the Local Defence Volunteers. This title, however, was unpopular and in mid-1940 they became the Home Guard. There were twenty-four Home Guard battalions in Sussex. Each battalion grew to a strength of 1,700 men, with each platoon consisting of 40 men.

Typical of these battalions was the 20th Sussex (Hailsham) Battalion formed in May 1940 under Lieutenant-Colonel R.H. Johnson DSO. Platoon commanders were given lists of men in their districts who had reported as volunteers to local police stations. Once enrolled, training commenced with Regular Army procedures. They mounted night observation posts on the highest point in their locality, usually church towers, and also guarded public services like telephone offices and assisted during ARP calls. The 20th Sussex Battalion operated over a wide area, bordered by rural Alfriston, Laughton, Heathfield, Boreham Street and Wartling. On 27 April 1943 women were allowed to join the Home Guard and the 20th Sussex was restricted to 56 females. Often Home Guard units were formed from staff within factories or public offices to protect the buildings.

The so-called 'Lewes Cossacks' unit was formed from men employed in the county town's racing fraternity. Based at the racecourse stables, the cavalry section consisted of 52 volunteers who served with considerable verve patrolling the Downs, where vehicular access was problematic. A similar cavalry group operated on the South Downs from Storrington, where the unofficial 'Horse Patrol' was led by Colonel Thynne of Muntham Court.

The Home Guard was disbanded on 11 November 1944. At its peak it numbered 1,084 battalions.

The stern but confident expressions of these Lindfield Home Guard volunteers also convey some apprehension about their role in the defence of the nation. (*W. Marchant*)

The Humber 8cwt GS was built specifically for military usage and was the only four-wheel-drive British vehicle at the time. This model was also a great success and 6,500 versions were produced with utility, ambulance and personnel carrier bodywork. (*Gote House*)

With the advent of hostilities many tourist attractions, like the novel Romney, Hythe & Dymchurch Railway in Kent, were enlisted for military use. Here a posed scene shows a variety of light guns positioned on the 15-in gauge light railway trucks. In essence, though, they may have provided a predictable target for the enemy! The RH&DR engine *Hercules* and two converted hopper wagons were adapted to patrol the 13 miles of railway line and a special military timetable was put into operation so that supplies and soldiers could be ferried along the coast. After the war the railway was in poor condition, but was partially re-opened in 1946 after a huge effort by staff, local people and former Italian prisoners of war. (*Gote House*)

At the outbreak of hostilities some 26,000 civilian vehicles were requisitioned by the Army, including 5,000 private cars, 14,000 motor-cycles and about 7,000 trucks. The War Department retained 55,000 vehicles, including all the civilian stock. A large number of these vehicles were sent to France with the British Expeditionary Force and were lost with the Dunkirk evacuations the following spring. Many modest family cars, like the restored Hillman Minx (seen above with RAF Wartling emblazoned on the door), became vital to national communications. (*Gote House*)

A total of 13,102 Austin K2 lorries were made between August 1939 and June 1945. Mann Egerton fabricated the wooden-framed and canvas-covered bodywork. The overall sturdy format was deemed a highly successful design and many thousands of these trucks were sold to other countries. (*Gote House*)

SHOREHAM AERODROME, 1940S

Several defence posts of unique design remain around the perimeter of Shoreham airfield. These relics of the 1940s aerodrome are alongside the River Adur and a busy civilian airfield – vivid reminders of Second World War activities. (*Gote House*)

The anti-aircraft gun dome trainer, Type 73/42, at Shoreham is a rare survivor and now receives sympathetic maintenance in accordance with its Listed category. Trainee gunners plotted images screened around the inner walls. (*Gote House*)

Shoreham airfield, with its grass landing strips, dates from 1911. Several runway patterns and many trading groups have functioned there over the years. The charismatic Art Deco Terminal Building opened officially in June 1936 and now carries a Listed category. (*Gote House*)

The aerodrome's northern guard-house bears vivid evidence of rebuilding, not camouflage. A USAAF Flying Fortress bomber careered into the property on 11 February 1944, killing an RAF detainee therein. The B-17 crew escaped serious injury. (*Gote House*)

Surviving wartime mural art varies in quality from the naive to the expert. Examples are noted at St Elisabeth's Church in Eastbourne, St Michael and All Angels at Berwick, at Michelham Priory and Newhaven Fort. Soldiers' colourful artwork adorns the walls of the gymnasium at Sussex University's White House Training Centre at the Isle of Thorns, Chelwood Gate, near Crowborough. Parish records describe the men as being from the London Irish Rifles TA. They played the pipes and drums and wore green jackets and orange kilts. The scenes depict weary troops during winter, longing to get back home. Troops in transit occupied what was then the Isle of Thorns Boys Camp created by East Grinstead philanthropist Alfred Wragg in the 1930s. (*Gote House*)

The imposing St Elisabeth's Church in Victoria Drive, Eastbourne, was completed in the late 1930s and features simplistic details of the late Art Deco era. Structural faults were overlooked after the war but eventually became so serious that the church was due for demolition in 1998. (*Gote House*)

However, St Elisabeth's was saved from demolition because it contains some Grade II Listed 1944 artwork. Refugee artist Hans Feibusch created life-size portrayals from John Bunyan's classic book *Pilgrim's Progress* around the crypt walls. In addition to this work Mr Feibusch undertook other commissions, like his *Nativity* scene at St Wilfrid's in Elm Grove, Brighton, in 1940. (*Gote House*)

The twelfth-century village church of St Michael and All Angels of Berwick, near Alfriston, has a beautiful series of murals to remind visitors of the area's military past. After many of the church windows were blown out during air raids the Church Council negotiated the addition of murals around the inner walls, painted by members of the Bloomsbury Set farming nearby at Charleston Manor. To the left of the chancel arch Duncan Grant created the kneeling figures of three servicemen: Douglas Hemming, a soldier killed at Caen in 1944, Mr Weller, a sailor, and Mr Humphrey, an airman. At the altar, depictions of the disciples are modelled on RAAF men quartered in the county. The murals were dedicated by Bishop Bell of Chichester in October 1943. (*Gote House*)

On 21 April 1998 the renowned aviation artist Frank Wootton OBE died at his Alfriston home, aged 88. Two weeks later his funeral was held at Berwick church and 200 mourners attended. A solitary Spitfire roared overhead in tribute to his contributions to aviation art and the community. (*Gote House*)

Pillboxes remain the most obvious artefacts of the Second World War across Sussex. They were constructed between mid-1940 and April 1941, when army commanders decided that they preferred earthwork defences for civilian locations. This elaborate circular two-storey pillbox survives near Bodiam, beside the B2244 road-bridge, to protect the Rother. (*Gote House*)

A rare survivor of wartime Stanton sectional hutting is to be found near Camber Castle, where a searchlight post and aerial decoy lighting system were located. (*Gote House*)

The Bofors gun tower near Gatwick lasted until the late 1990s when it was felled during site development. Some original mainfast fittings are seen intact on the top of the platform. (*Gote House*)

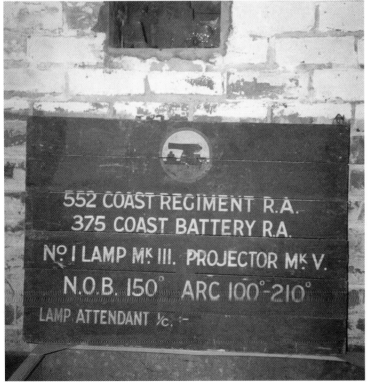

Relics of no. 375 Coast Battery can be seen at Norman's Bay sluice between Pevensey and Bexhill. Two searchlight posts were created either side of the pair of 4.7-inch First World War naval guns, of Japanese origin, allocated to the battery. Beach Crest bungalow was requisitioned by no. 552 Coast Regiment of the Royal Artillery just after it was built in mid-1940. The Army erected the adjoining brick searchlight post as no. 1, with the eastern searchlight post on the beach (in a now extended white bungalow). Papers on the battery have been found in the PRO. At other locations dummy domestic property camouflaged military posts. (*Gote House*)

Former RNAS Peregrine aerodrome buildings at Ford Junction have been adapted to accommodate inmates at HM Prison Ford. (*Gote House*)

This gazebo relic of Splash Point Hotel at Seaford shows signs of being used during the Second World War. The reinforced concrete roof platform and period brickwork suggest it became a lookout or light machine-gun post. (*Gote House*)

It can be exhilerating exploring sites and installations and a pair of gun bases (one of which is on the right) can be seen near Hellingly Hospital. In the 1940s the hospital was used as an Army Medical Corps casualty unit. (*Gote House*)

Memories of barrack life, of comradeship, of regulations and routine, off NCOs and other ranks, and of escapades from the time of the Second World War and National Service remain indelibly implanted in the minds of many ex-servicemen. (*Alan Pearson*)

Kit inspection, parades and close attention to detail are recalled in this reconstruction. (*Newhaven Fort*)

Sussex is blessed with bizarre properties from all eras. Bishopstone station was built in 1937–8 in Art Deco style to service the proposed light industrial development of the now residential area. The pair of wartime roof-top pillboxes were possibly added a year or two later, and blended in nicely with the splendid modernistic styling of the station. (*Gote House*)

The pebble-walled hamlet of Bishopstone Tide Mills was devastated after war broke out. Buildings were demolished to create a clear field of fire because they could have provided the enemy with landing cover. The site of the village was given over to urban warfare training grounds. (*Gote House*)

Mill Drove, the Tide Mills, High Street, was metalled as a tank road to take tanks and troops to the beaches. (*Gote House*)

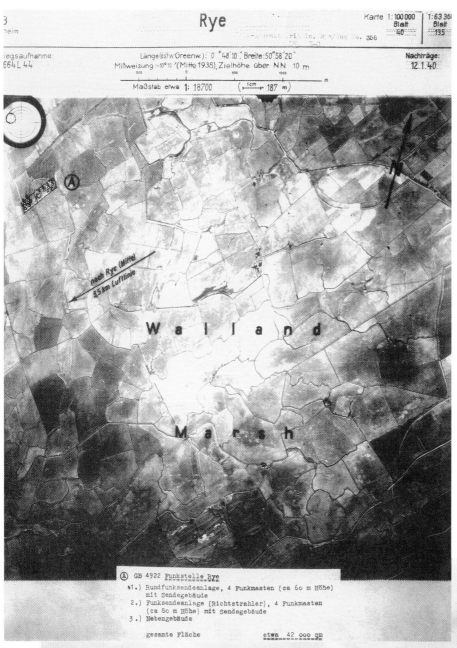

Rye

| Karte 1:100 000 Blatt | 1:63 360 Blatt |
| 40 | 135 |

Länge (östl. Greenw.): 0°48'10'', Breite: 50°58'20''
Mißweisung :–10°10' (Mitte 1938), Zielhöhe über NN 10 m
Maßstab etwa 1: 18700   (1 cm → 187 m)

Nachträge:
12.1.40.

W a l l a n d

M a r s h

nach Rye (Mitte)
5,5 km Luftlinie

Ⓐ GB 4922 Funkstelle Rye

1.) Rundfunksendeanlage, 4 Funkmasten (ca 60 m Höhe)
    mit Sendegebäude
2.) Funksendeanlage (Richtstrahler), 4 Funkmasten
    (ca 80 m Höhe) mit Sendegebäude
3.) Nebengebäude

gesamte Fläche   etwa 42 000 qm

The masts of RAF Rye radar station can be seen at top left, along with their shadows, in this Luftwaffe reconnaissance photograph taken over Walland Marsh in January 1940. (*Nigel J. Clarke*)

A feature of the Chain Home radar buildings is the darker brick used on the roofs of the units. The walls retained layers of gravel protection, to absorb impact, after bombing. Radar stations from Ventnor to Dover were attacked by Stuka Ju87 dive-bombers at around 0900 hours on 12 August 1940, but otherwise the AMES sites escaped virtually unscathed, despite their importance in detecting enemy aircraft. They were initially dubbed Air Ministry Experimental Stations to conceal their real purpose. (*Gote House*)

An airman's eye-view over Seaford Head in 1945. The groynes are now buried under shingle and urban development brown field in-fill has overtaken the once sprawling township. Seaford suffered a considerable amount of enemy aerial attention – twenty-two people were killed outright, including Chief ARP Controller Mr W.P. Tomley. (*Gote House*)

This little pillbox has survived the postwar years on Seaford seafront as a groundsman's shed. It formerly served with the no. 521 Coastal Regiment battery nearby. (*Gote House*)

The stretch of exposed beach between Pevensey Bay and Norman's Bay hosts a variety of holiday chalets, many of which utilise wartime anti-invasion blocks as foundation-bearers. (*Gote House*)

Sixty years on and wartime debris still litters our beaches. Here, Pierced Steel Planking (PSP), metal tank tracking used to support heavy transport and aircraft over uncertain surfaces, lies redundant and rusting on shingle wasteland at Pevensey. (*Gote House*)

In February 1940 evacuees from the Medway towns of Rochester and Strood took up residence in a specially constructed National Camps Corporation Ltd hutted camp at Wrens Warren on Ashdown Forest. The timber school buildings survived as storage units until early 2001 when they made way for private homes. In January 2001 many of the former evacuee children were reunited at the heathland site. (East Grinstead Observer)

During the Second World War landmarks that might have aided enemy navigators were concealed. The outline of the mysterious Long Man of Wilmington, 230 ft tall, was painted over. (Gote House)

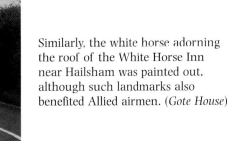

Similarly, the white horse adorning the roof of the White Horse Inn near Hailsham was painted out, although such landmarks also benefited Allied airmen. (Gote House)

IT'S NEW!
IT'S NEWS!
IT'S—

Butlin's OCEAN HOTEL

SALTDEAN · BRIGHTON · SUSSEX

- ☼ All-in tariff on the Butlin Plan
- ☼ Lovely Swimming Pool and Splashpo
- ☼ Magnificent Ballroom overlooking the Sea
- ☼ Licensed Lounges and Bars for Residents only
- ☼ Open all the Year—solely for Holidays
- ☼ Central Heating and Constant Hot Water in every bedroom
- ☼ 400 Rooms 140 Bathrooms Free Car Park

OPENING MAY 2ND 1953

CONTINENTAL-STYLE Seaside Resort Hotel with glass-enclosed sundecks—a sunbather's paradise!

NOTHING like this has ever been known before—anywhere! A great hotel run on the lines of a Butlin holiday camp—with good food, central heating and constant hot water in every bedroom, all the entertainment you could wish for, all the sport and *all the sunshine*. That is what Butlin's, and only Butlin's, can offer you at an "All-in" tariff in 1953. The magnificent Ocean Hotel, designed to catch

the sun's rays, with its marvellous terraces and roof-garden sundecks surrounded by glass screens, is gloriously situated on the lovely Sussex coast, looking out over the English Channel. It offers virtually the same amenities as a Butlin camp *plus* the thrill of a "land-cruise" and the comfort of an up-to-the-minute self-contained hotel. This **Special Booking Form** comes to you before the opening is announced in the newspapers—complete it *now* and—

—MAKE SURE OF A WONDERFUL HOLIDAY!

CONDITIONS OF RESERVATION

BEDROOMS. Are equipped for two, or three, persons. Therefore, it is most important, when applying for accommodation for more than one person, that the degree of relationship is inserted in the appropriate column in Section 3 (i.e. husband, wife, daughter, son or friend). This information is necessary for allocating to your party the most suitable type of bedroom available. If only one person is applying or if any members of the party cannot be accommodated in one bedroom, it is understood that he, she or they would be agreeable to share a bedroom (separate beds) with persons of the same age and sex. Bedrooms for single occupancy—see Section 5.

HOLIDAY CLUB. At each Butlin establishment is a Holiday Club, membership of which is essential to enable guests to participate in the many facilities. These include dancing, cabarets, tennis, games, etc. The persons named overleaf request nomination for election as Country Members of the BUTLIN (OCEAN HOTEL) HOLIDAY CLUB. The Membership Fee of 1/- is included in the tariff.

CHILDREN'S AGES. The age group of all children must be clearly indicated. No children under two years of age can be accepted at any time, and during the months of July and August, no children under the age of 14 years can be accommodated.

RATION BOOKS. It is necessary for Ration Books to be tendered on arrival by residents staying for FIVE NIGHTS OR LONGER.

PETS. Dogs, cats or other pets cannot be admitted.

DEPOSITS. The deposit is a Booking Fee. In the event of you being unable to take your holiday with us owing to circumstances beyond the control of Butlin's Limited, the Booking Fee will be forfeited. However, in such an event, providing notice of cancellation is given in writing at least TWENTY-ONE DAYS prior to the date of arrival, or by production of a Medical Certificate in the case of illness, a voucher will be sent to you for 50% of the amount of deposit for use as a deposit for a holiday at the Ocean Hotel at a future date.

Applicants undertake to relieve the Management of all liability whatsoever for accidents to themselves and/or for the loss of or damage to their property.

The Management reserves the right to decline accommodation. The Company is relieved from liability should the accommodation not be available due to any circumstances whatsoever.

GUESTS ARE REQUESTED TO BRING THEIR OWN TOWELS AND SOAP. LUGGAGE MAY BE SENT IN ADVANCE.

Inside the Ocean Hotel, a week after its opening in July 1938. Wartime priorities over-shadowed the gaiety as commandeering plans were already in place. (*Gote House*)

After adoption in 1939 as an evacuee centre for expectant mothers from London the hotel was taken over as the National Fire College during the war. After refurbishment it was relaunched as Butlin's Ocean Hotel on 2 May 1953. (*Gote House*)

SUBURBAN SALTDEAN AT WAR ON THE OCEAN HOTEL

The development of downland between Brighton and Newhaven between the wars was led by Charles Neville's garden-city-by-the-sea ideals for Peacehaven and Telscombe. By the mid-1930s the hilly terrain now known as Saltdean was being developed and notable homes in the area were built in the popular Art Deco style. Significant properties included Saltdean Lido on the coast road and the £200,000 Ocean Hotel with its 426 bedrooms, designed by the renowned architect R.W.H. Jones, who was elected a Fellow of the Royal Institute of Architects in 1939. Administration of the district has been variably in the hands of Brighton Borough Council, Chailey Rural District Council, Newhaven Town Council and Lewes District Council.

The Ocean Hotel was devised in such a way that off-season the six detached blocks could be shut down and the main building of 130 bedrooms operated as a separate hotel. It opened in July 1938.

With evacuation of coastal communities being discussed as early as 1937 it may be surprising that the nationally organised evacuation programme, which swiftly swung into place, designated large numbers of evacuees to be settled in Sussex's coastal towns. Initially the Ocean Hotel was occupied by refugee pregnant mothers from London, but during the phoney war in late 1939 and early 1940 many evacuees drifted back to their homes in the capital. Later plans detailed evacuation of people away from the coastal districts.

In December 1939 the Ocean Hotel was commandeered by the ATS (Auxiliary Territorial Service, later the Women's Royal Army Corps) after the number of evacuees diminished. On 10 October 1941 Herbert Morrison, the Home Secretary, opened the premises as a National Fire Service College – the first of its kind in the country – at a time when the demands on the Fire Brigade were anticipated to expand twenty-fold.

DEVASTATION AND RESURRECTION

As the new regime took over the once palatial hotel, internal alterations followed and the college facilities became quite self-contained. Outside, in civilian Saltdean, a number of aircraft incidents and numerous army exercises continued to alarm the community situated on the cliff tops east of Brighton. A Housewives Home Guard unit was formed and a Self-Help Fellowship accommodated communal needs during the war. Rolling downland bordering the suburb was used for intensive artillery and army training.

Utilisation of the hotel by the National Fire Service continued for many years after the war, although local social organisations also made use of its facilities. There were various rumours associated with the sprawling premises. The front-page story in the *Peacehaven and Newhaven Times* dated 24 January 1947 claimed that the hotel was up for sale at £500,000. The suggestion that it was to be used as an open prison heightened anxiety in the district and it was a great relief when (Sir) Billy Butlin's holiday organisation purchased the hotel for a quarter of a million pounds – the entrepreneur later declared it was the best deal he ever made.

The newly formed Saltdean Community Association presented its major event on New Year's Day 1949. Over 350 guests braved the weather to enjoy the dance staged at the Ocean Hotel. It took a team of workmen six months to renovate the near-derelict hotel, and its doors were opened once again to the public on 2 May 1953, as Coronation gaiety seized the nation.

St Giles' Church at Horsted Keynes, near Haywards Heath, is usually remembered as the last resting place of former Prime Minister Harold Macmillan and members of his family. But this graveyard also contains the only Commonwealth War Graves Commission headstone bearing a pair of military cap badges. WAAF Corporal Winifred Ellen Knapp of Horsted Keynes and Gunner Ronald Knapp were married on 31 July 1943 at St Giles. Taking a short cut home from the reception, they were walking by a railway line when they were tragically struck by a train during a thunderstorm. (*Michael Grainger*)

This National Trust sign on Ditchling Beacon commemorates the death of Flying Officer Richard Demitriadi, of 601 Squadron, while piloting Hurricane R4092 off Portland on 1 August 1940. Sir Stephen Demitriadi KBE donated the headland in memory of his youngest son who gave his life during the Battle of Britain. (*Gote House*)

Neat rows of German aircrew graves in the grounds of St Andrew's Church at Tangmere. (*Gote House*)

Clearance of military training terrain on the Downs was a priority in postwar Sussex. Reinstatement plans had already been prepared and military authorities were pressured to release land back to civilian control. It is interesting to note how many old cart-tracks and bridle-ways were metalled to allow military vehicles access to the Downs. (*East Sussex Record Office*)

TO :—

TELEPHONE: **The Clerk of the County Council**
BRIGHTON 5944 & 5945.   **County Hall, LEWES.**

J. LORD THOMPSON & WEEKS
SOLICITORS.   BRIGHTON SAVINGS BANK CHAMBERS,
WM. E. WEEKS.   30, NEW ROAD,
COMMISSIONER FOR OATHS.   WW/DB   BRIGHTON, 1.

                               22nd May 1946.

Dear Sir,
        re South Downs Preservation Military
        Roads TB/PH.
        ————

        Your communication of the 24th ult., has reached me. As you are aware the Dyke Golf Club is not at present functioning, owing to having been taken over by the Military Authorities.

        Although it is not possible to walk over the whole of the Dyke Golf Course at the present time, owing to its dangerous condition, the Course not having been cleared, so far as I can ascertain there are no roads on the Course which have been either constructed or improved. There may be certain rough tracks which have been used by military vehicles or tanks, but hardly distinguishable now as such.

        With regard to your question No. 2 I believe there is an existing bridle path which passes over one part of the Course, but this was little used before the war, and now owing to the dangerous state of the Downs, has not probably been used for several years.

        I shall be very interested now to know when it is likely to be de-requisitioned, and if we can do anything to assist or co-operate with this object in view, I shall be pleased to do so.
                Yours faithfully
                Wm. E. Weeks
                Hon. Secretary Dyke Golf Club

Ministry of Town & Country Planning.

Our Ref: SE/GEN/355 HRW/MTS.   Regional Planning Office,
Your ref: 24, Calverley Park,
                                       Tunbridge Wells.
                                       Kent.
                                       10th December, 1945.

Dear Humphery,

        South Downs Training Area – Roads.

    Atkins has now completed his observations on the roads so far as he is able. Unfortunately, owing to the presence of unexploded ammunition, he has not been able to do more than the approach roads. We must wait until the area is tidied up before we can get on to a survey of the interior.

    So far as he has gone a summary of his conclusions on the various roads is as follows :—

    Road No.1 Clayton Holt. (Eastern Area) Metalling to be taken up and road to be allowed to its original condition.

    Road No.2 Plumpton Plain. Road to be left to revert to its original condition. Consideration to be given to the question of providing a gate near its lower end, with a gap at one side for ped-estrians and riders.

    Road No.3 Telscombe. No action necessary. Road to be left to revert to its original condition.

    Road No.8 Seaford Head. Consideration to be given to the possibility of retaining the concrete approach roads, and providing a fenced car park at South Hill Barn. The concrete branch roads and loops to be broken up and the ground restored to its original condition.

    Road No.4 Beddingham Hill. Road to be left to revert to its original condition. A gate to be provided above the junction with the track to "The Furlongs". Soil to be spread over all exposed chalk if practicable.

    Road No.5 West Firle. Road to be left to revert to its original condition. A gate to be set up by the cottage south of "Newelm". Soil be spread over all exposed chalk if practicable.

    Road No.6 Bopeep. Alciston. Road to be left to revert to its original condition. A gate to be provided just South of Bopeep Farm. Soil to be spread over all exposed chalk if practicable.

    Road No.7 Winton Lane, Alfriston. (Below Winton Chalk Pit) Consideration to be given to the question of providing a gate just above "The Sanctuary".

    (Winton Chalk Pit to summit) W.D. to be asked to remove metalling entirely, fill in, smooth over soil or turf, thereby restoring the hillside to its original state.

    We should be glad to have your observations upon the matter as soon as you are able to let us have them.

                Yours sincerely,
                (Signed) H.R.WARDILL
                Regional Planning Officer.

NOTE: The location of each road has been added for convenience.

Built in 1933 by William Denny & Sons of Dumbarton for the Southern Railway, the SS *Brighton* is seen here in Seaford Bay in its prime, en route between Newhaven and Dieppe. It was one of many vessels chartered by the Admiralty as hospital ships or military transports. On 24 May 1940 the vessel became a war loss, despite bearing Red Cross markings. It was scuttled after being attacked alongside a hospital train in Dieppe harbour with the *Maid of Kent*, prior to the Operation Dynamo evacuations. The ships were blocked in the harbour, and amazingly nobody was killed in the Luftwaffe attack. (Photograph above: *Austin Williamson*)

A chance encounter some sixty years later led to the discovery of the ship's bell from SS *Brighton*. Local publisher Steve Benz noticed the bell in a Warwick antique shop during a business trip. Mr Benz purchased the sole surviving artefact of the SS *Brighton* and presented it to Newhaven Historical Society. It is now on display at their Avis Road museum. (Photograph below: *reproduced by kind permission of the* Sussex Express)

MILITARY TRANSPORT VESSELS

The single-funnelled cross-Channel ferry SS *Worthing* was built for the Southern Railway in 1928 by William Denny & Bros of Dumbarton. She sailed continually between Newhaven and Dieppe at the height of the boom era of overseas excursions and could carry 900 passengers. At the outbreak of war she was requisitioned and carried British Expeditionary Force troops to France. In November 1939 she was converted to hospital carrier no. 30 and commenced crossings between Newhaven and Dieppe from 7 January 1940.

On 26 May she was sent to Dunkirk and brought back 600 men in two crossings. On 2 June she left again for Dunkirk and this time, despite bearing hospital markings, she was attacked by a dozen aircraft. Nine bombs struck the vessel. Taking water, she was forced back to Newhaven. On 11 June she sailed to Le Havre and carried casualties to Newhaven. Then she went to Southampton and she was converted into a Fleet Air Arm target vessel and commissioned as HMS *Worthing* on 13 November.

On 7 December she was renamed HMS *Brigadier* and went to the Firth of Forth as a target vessel for Crail Naval Air Station. In May 1942 she was converted at West Hartlepool into an infantry landing ship. After training exercises she was in the Solent by 5 June 1944, to take part in the assault convoy for Juno Beach at Normandy. Later she joined the Allied fleet ferrying supplies to the continent.

In March 1945 the former SS *Worthing* returned to peacetime ferry duties from Newhaven and was refitted in 1946 for civilian service. In 1955 the vessel was sold for ferry trade between Piraeus and Crete and was finally broken up in 1964.

HMS *Broadwater*, named after the Worthing suburb, was in the news again in mid-2000 when a special award was organised to commemorate a wartime tragedy. Caffyns Ltd endowed an award named the HMS *Broadwater* Trophy to be presented annually to the best history student in a Worthing school.

HMS *Broadwater* was sunk on 18 October 1941 while escorting a British cargo convoy south-west of Iceland. Forty-five seamen perished when the vessel was torpedoed. A memorial service was held at St Mary's Church at Broadwater, where a plaque perpetuated the memory of the men who lost their lives in the sinking of the vessel.

The wartime role of HMS *Plumpton* is depicted on the walls of the Half Moon Inn at rural Plumpton under the Downs near Lewes. A photograph of the ship and details of her career are vivid reminders of the extensive range of naval duties during times of war.

HMS *Lewes* is recorded on the walls of the Lewes Arms in Mount Place, Lewes. The ship's crest was presented by the Admiralty to the town to commemorate its adoption of HMS *Lewes* during Warship Week 1942. The crest is now on permanent loan from Lewes District Council to the public house.

HMS *Lewes* was a four-stack destroyer launched as the USS *Conway* on 29 June 1918. She was issued to the Royal Navy in 1940. HMS *Lewes* served in the Home Fleet (1940–1), in the South Atlantic (1942–4) and in the Pacific Fleet (1945). Her long career ended off Australia in 1946 when she was ordered to be scuttled.

Interestingly, the crest at the Lewes Arms actually depicts that of the Lord of the Isles (Lewis in Scotland) – an error seemingly made under the pressure of wartime.

The lush Devil's Dyke headland near Brighton is actually in the parish of Poynings. During the Second World War the area was on the edge of Zone 8: South Downs Training Area (East), as shown on 1940 Army sheet no. 134. Although local authorities promptly cleared the area of ammunition and war effects and reopened the land to the public again, a few signs of military use still remain to this day. This photograph shows the foundations of a brick observation post on the ramparts of an Iron Age defensive earthwork, close to a trigonometry point. Elsewhere soil mounds, ditches and fox-holes indicate the activities of sixty years ago. The Devil's Dyke Hotel lay derelict until 1954, after being burned out in 1946 by exuberant troops. The current hotel was built in 1967. (*Gote House*)

The glazed brick frontage to this secret dug-out is hidden away in a quarry near the eastern end of the Devil's Dyke gorge. A sign on the waste land used to bear the Brighton Corporation crest. The cave was reportedly where Brighton Council hid its documents in case of invasion. In subsequent years the entrance was concealed with chalk deposits, although youths would often open the passage-way. More recently it has been used as a WSCC reserve for bats, but once again the dark corridors and rooms appear abandoned. (*Gote House*)

Aviation archaeology now has an avid following, although excavation at crash sites is carefully regulated. There is, however, a great deal of research to carry out regarding wartime incidents and relics are still being uncovered. Right: a USAAF B-17 propellor dredged up at Eastbourne Marina. (*Gote House*). Below: the author examines RAF Dakota wreckage found near the Long Man of Wilmington. (*Gote House*)

Bottom left: the Rolls-Royce Merlin excavated at Phil Wooller's farm. On 5 May 1942 Spitfire VB BM375, flown by Pilot Officer Edward Hall, crashed into a meadow at Underwood Farm, Wilmington, with a glycol leak. The pilot parachuted to safety and revisited the site in 1978. In 1986 farmer Phil Wooller, a young man at the time of the crash, helped to dig out the wreckage of the Spitfire. Its Rolls-Royce Merlin engine was ferried by helicopter to the Redoubt Museum in Eastbourne, where it remains on display. (*Phil Wooller*). Bottom right: curious 1940s alloy aircraft sections found among gorse near the Long Man of Wilmington. (*Gote House*)

Naval mines were a notorious hazard to shipping during the Second World War. Eventually many broke loose and were washed up on the shore. After the war some served as collection points for charitable causes. Top left: an unmarked mine on Hastings promenade. (*Gote House*) Top right: the restored mine on display at Eastbourne Redoubt Museum. Middle: the mine at Rye harbour remains in use, collecting for the Shipwrecked Mariners Society. (*Gote House*) Bottom: this mine was washed along the tidal Cuckmere river, travelling some 4 miles inland, in October 1943. A naval team rendered the mine harmless and it remains on Alfriston Tye as a village fund-raising source. (*Gote House*)

Alfriston High Street in the 1940s, photographed from the Market Place cross. Officers relax as Bren-gun carriers pass by. Downland around the village was alive with troops on gunnery and training exercises prior to embarkation. Left: did the scene above the second vehicle inspire the lyrics of 'How Much is that Doggie in the Window'? (*Patricia Berry*)

The same scene today, where visitors from many nations meet in cordial recreation. (*Gote House*)

The imposing Art Deco-style St Dunstan's Centre, Ovingdean. (*Gote House*)

ST DUNSTAN'S

St Dunstan's, Ovingdean, the centre for blind ex-servicemen and servicewomen, dominates the A259 coast-road, cliff-top approach from Brighton.

Sir Arthur Pearson, the newspaper magnate, founded St Dunstan's in 1915 to care for those blinded in the First World War. The first training centre and workshop was situated in a large house in Regent's Park, London. The charity took its name from the house already called St Dunstan's, which was named after a clock in the grounds and this originally came from the Church of St Dunstan-in-the-West in Fleet Street.

In 1918 a property in Kemp Town (Brighton) called West House (subsequently renamed Pearson House) was presented to St Dunstan's by the Federation of Grocers Association. Until the 1995 sale of that property it was used for training, but also operated as a nursing, residential and a holiday home. By the late 1930s the house was becoming inadequate. With the possibility of another war looming, and the anticipation of a great influx of blinded service personnel, it was agreed that another property should be acquired.

The decision was made to construct a new purpose-built centre on a downland site at Ovingdean, which had been made available by Brighton Corporation. The prize-winning Art Deco-style complex was commissioned from Francis Lorne, who designed one of the most striking examples of modern architecture at that time. The building resembled an aeroplane in outline and was noted for the amount of external glass. Its primary aim was to permit the greatest possible volume of sunshine inside the building for the occupants to enjoy.

The new building was completed in 1938. Ovingdean became a hospital and training centre for the newly blind servicemen and servicewomen. In 1940 St Dunstan's was deemed to be in too dangerous a position on the south coast. Under the direction of Sir Ian Fraser, who had been in the chair following the death of Sir Arthur Pearson in 1921, St Dunstan's moved to Church Stretton in Shropshire for the duration of the war and returned to Brighton in 1946. Meanwhile, the Admiralty took over the house and it became part of HMS *Vernon*, a naval school for instruction in under-water weapons.

Since the end of the Second World War the Ovingdean centre has gone from strength to strength, undergoing many internal alterations to keep pace with changing needs and expectations. In 1971 it was renamed Ian Fraser House in honour of the chairman's fifty years in office. In 1995 its name reverted to St Dunstan's Ovingdean following the sale of Pearson House. Today the centre provides training, rehabilitation, nursing, respite and residential care and holidays for blind ex-servicemen and servicewomen.

THE VENGEANCE BOMB TERROR

The V1, or *Vergeltungswaffe* 1, Vengeance bomb attack on the British mainland commenced on 6 June 1944 – just hours after the D-Day landings in enemy-occupied France. The daunting sound of the pilotless jet-pulse can be recalled by many people, like a noisy airborne motor-cycle. When the engine died it simply crashed to earth.

The nation had been heavily battered by the Battle of Britain in 1940, followed by the 1940–1 Blitz and night raids on towns and rural areas. After the relief and glory of the D-Day landings the V1 retaliation caused a severe blow to the nation's morale, and some 5,500 people died as a result of the jet-powered bomb attacks. Night and day the V1s rained terror over southern England. Although most were aimed at the capital, many fell short of their target or were intercepted by the gun barrage and aerial balloon barrage around London. The brave Allied pilots of the RAF now fought a new battle over the southern counties: intercepting the pilotless flying bombs, they attempted to tip their wings to turn them back out to sea. Alas, all too often the RAF sustained heavy losses in these dangerous manoeuvres.

The V1 pulse-jet flying bomb was known at the time as a diver, a fly or more popularly a doodlebug. At 25 ft 4 in long, they had a wingspan of 17 ft 6 in and were constructed from sheet steel and plywood.

The ferocious flying bomb attacks engendered an intense campaign for Allied troops advancing through Europe to take over launch sites. Meanwhile in Britain the casualty list grew and grew. Some 121 people died during morning service at the Guards Chapel in London. A bomb falling in The Aldwych caused 48 fatalities, and 74 died in US Army billets in Sloane Square after a direct hit. A total of 2,419 V1s fell on London, and killed 5,126 people; 2,789 flying bombs fell outside London and 350 people died as a result.

The onslaught only lessened when the Allied defences across southern counties gradually assumed superiority. But it all changed in September 1944 when the 3,600mph V2 long-range rocket attacks commenced.

It was Kent that bore the brunt of the V1 onslaught. Some 1,444 Vengeance bombs fell there – more than fell on London itself. It is estimated that a thousand V1s crashed into the sea off Kent and caused damage to coastal properties. Records show that 775 bombs fell in East Sussex, with the more easterly areas suffering the greatest numbers. None fell in Brighton, Hove, Portslade, or inland around Burgess Hill. Battle Rural District bore the brunt of the V1 Operation *Kirschkern* (Cherrystone) campaign. Only four V2 rockets fell in Sussex.

Numerous robust relics of wartime defence remain as countryside curios. This former gun emplacement near Upper Beeding has been made into a rural feature beside the River Adur. (*Gote House*)

The V1 doodlebug and V2 rocket onslaught almost turned the tide of warfare against Britain. Brave pilots trained to intercept them and change their direction – all too often such encounters led to the pilot's death. Most famous of the aircraft that went into combat against the V1s were the Hawker Tempest, capable of 420mph, and the Spitfire F-XIV Griffon 65. The North American Mustang also joined the fray, as did the venerable de Havilland Mosquito. On 4 August 1944 Britain's first jet fighter, the 485mph Gloster Meteor, took on anti-V1 duties. Numerous doodlebug components can be found in museums and private collections. Few remain, however, where they fell – as is the case with this debris in private woodland near Mayfield. (*Gote House*)

A 3.7-in heavy gun battery, part of the coastal gun barrage at West Marina, St Leonards, mid–1944. The extensive gun belt was extended inland from Beachy Head to Dover and was supported by barrage balloons and fighter aircraft scrambled to intercept enemy aircraft. (*Gote House*)

On 3 August 1944 a doodlebug fell close to Tidebrook School, near Marks Cross. Mercifully pupils had taken shelter in time. No serious injuries resulted from this attack, although the bomb landed just 25 yards from the school. It was never rebuilt and the former school house is now a private home. A plaque in Tidebrook Church commemorates the day the schoolchildren survived the V1 raid. The plaque erroneously states that the incident happened on 4 August. (*Gote House*)

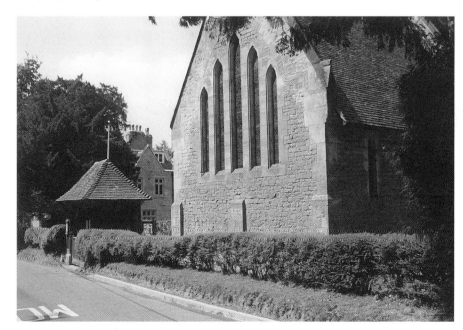

DOODLEBUG DIARY

13 June 1944. The second V1 to fall in the UK was reported down at Misbrooks Farm, **Cuckfield**, at 4.20am. Army and Air Ministry boffins were soon at the scene. Nominal damage was caused and the bomb seemed 'confused' as it came from the direction of London and circled around the countryside before falling on the village. In total 23 flying bombs were to fall in the district.

16 June. A doodlebug crashed at Riverside Nurseries at Marle Green, **Horam**.

17 June. Extensive damage to Possingworth Park Hotel and some houses at **Waldron** resulted from a V1 that fell at 10.30pm. A cottage on the Southover Estate at **Mountfield** was demolished that same day, 2 minutes before midnight.

19 June. A V1 that crashed just before 11.00pm damaged property at Richmond Road, **Bexhill**, and caused a 30-ft-deep crater. For the greater part of 80 days Bexhill lay in the notorious 'bomb alley' flight path to London. At the height of the raids no fewer than 480 doodlebugs were tracked over Bexhill during a single 24-hour span – and many of them fell on the resort.

20 June. A flying bomb fell on **Herstmonceux** at 4.45am. At 6.45pm that day another crashed on the Southlands Estate at **Hailsham** and devastated 250 houses.

21 June. At 1.52am a doodlebug caused nominal damage to 174 properties at **Cadburgh Cliff. Icklesham** suffered at 1.55am and 8 properties sustained damage.

23 June. On the coast, **St Leonards** endured a doodlebug attack at 5.00am.

25 June. Church Street in **Willingdon** – on the outskirts of Eastbourne – incurred damage to a dozen properties at 3.45am. A total of 17 houses were devastated at **Staplehurst** in the parish of Ewhurst at 9.05pm.

26 June. Glovers Farm at **Sidley** sustained extensive damage at 3.52pm.

A Bofors anti-aircraft gun crew depicted ready for action. These mobile gun installations proved to be highly effective against aerial attack. (*Gote House*)

27 June. Poppinghole Farm at **Robertsbridge** reported a doodlebug attack at 8.36pm. At 6.50pm a V1 fell at Danegate Farm, **Rotherfield**.

29 June. Twenty houses sustained light damage at **Jevington**. At 11.55pm several houses in Military Road, **Playden**, were seriously damaged. Extensive destruction to 150 houses was reported at 6.55pm from the beach at **Pevensey**, where a V1 landed. Another crashed at Sandy Cross, **Heathfield**, at 9.00pm and some 50 houses were damaged.

30 June. At 3.10am a V1 crashed at **Maynards Gate**, Crowborough, resulting in severe damage to houses. At 8.43 **Ticehurst** Infirmary was severely damaged by another bomb.

1 July. At 1.50am a V1 fell at Springham Wood, **Hellingly**, and a dozen houses were devastated. At 7.30pm serious damage to a property at **Northiam** was reported.

3 July. At 0.53am 60 houses in Rye suffered damage when a V1 fell there. At 3.20pm Conqueror Road in **St Leonards** received a hit and at 6.55pm a V1 landed at Down Oak Farm, **Westfield**, demolishing a pair of homes. Also that day 54 houses were damaged by a V1 that fell at Potters Green, **Buxted**.

4 July. Cottages at **Udimore** were reported damaged by a V1 at 10.00am. Then at 3.45pm 6 houses at Northheath Farm, **Hailsham**, were hit. Over 40 properties were damaged at 7.30pm at West Street Lane, **Heathfield**.

5 July. Elms Farmhouse, **Iden**, was hit at 6.05pm. There were 10 Canadian soldiers killed when a V1 struck their camp on **Crowborough** golf course at 6.20pm.

6 July. At 1.04pm a V1 intruder at Mount Pleasant, **Newhaven**, damaged 30 houses, and another 75 homes at nearby **Denton** village were wrecked after a V1 attack.

7 July. At 11.45pm extensive damage to property was incurred at **Westfield**, Battle. The enemy had also struck at 4.15pm near Southlands Estate at **Polegate** inflicting extensive damage to 250 houses. At 4.30pm at nearby Plaquet Corner, **Arlington**, a home was demolished by a V1 and a woman died. At 5.00pm Prinkle Farm, **Dallington**, took a hit, damaging the farm and 50 shops and homes, while 18 properties were damaged when a V1 fell near Rennies Farm, **Isfield**. In addition there were 4 V1 fatalities at West Close, **Polegate**.

9 July. **Willingdon**, a suburb of Eastbourne, sustained blast damage to its church, school, memorial hall and some 50 homes at 11.50am. In all Eastbourne borough was to suffer 14 flying bomb attacks. At Woodlands Farm, **Balcombe**, a V1 devastated a farmhouse and out-buildings at 11.08pm and another fell at **Kings Standing** near Fairwarp at 11.25pm. Kings Standing was the location of the secret broadcasting bunker created for the Operation *Aspidistra* black propaganda programme.

10 July. Yew Tree Farm at **Punnets Town** near Heathfield was hit by a V1 at 10.55am and 21 properties were damaged. Mullbrooks House, **Hailsham**, suffered an attack at 4.56pm; 2 people died and 7 buildings were damaged. A flying bomb fell at the junction of Oak Road and West Street in **Crawley**, killing 7 people and seriously injuring 44 others; 15 homes were totally destroyed.

11 July. A V1 crashed into **Haywards Heath** cemetery grounds but no serious damage was recorded.

12 July. London Road in **East Grinstead** was attacked at 7.25am. As a result, 3 people died and over 400 properties were extensively damaged not far from the Whitehall cinema, where an attack the previous July resulted in 108 fatalities. At 8.40am Sharnden in **Mayfield** was devastated. That night at 9.15pm some 71 houses at **Rushlake Green** were damaged in an attack.

13 July. At 2.50pm Chapel Field, **Camber** was hit. The coastguard station and buildings were seriously damaged.

14 July. At 8.12am **Ticehurst** was attacked and 18 houses and farm buildings were damaged. At 5.54pm a house at Clanning Walk, **Cowden**, was demolished and others seriously damaged. A V1 fell between **Forest Row** and **Ashurst Wood**. It cut through power lines and struck a tree.

16 July. A bomb was reported down at Hollington, **Hastings** at 4.40pm. In all 15 flying bombs crashed in Hastings borough.

20 July. Some 23 buildings at **Burwash** sustained damage at 10.20am. Around 11.18pm another V1 crashed at Blatchington Golf Course, **Seaford**.

21 July. Burnt Oak Farm at **Waldron** was hit by a V1 at 9.25am.

22 July. A cottage at Tintern Lane in **Crowborough** was demolished when it was hit at 1.10am. Old Town in **Bexhill** was hit at 4.35pm and extensive damage to residences and businesses was reported. A flying bomb fell close to the **Uckfield** ARP Control Room and broke countless windows at council buildings. A fortnight later a V1 fell at Twitten Grange in **Uckfield**; it wrecked a couple of houses and damaged about 300 others. One person was killed. Overall 1,715 **Uckfield** Rural District properties sustained flying bomb damage and 23 properties were totally destroyed; 31 people were killed in the district. The first V2 reported in the district burst on to Rumsden Farm, **Crowborough**.

23 July. An early morning doodlebug raid at 6.00am demolished a farmhouse and 40 homes at **Chiddingly**. At 6.30am serious damage was reported at **Northiam**. There were 6 casualties, 2 of them fatal, caused when a V1 shot down by fighters struck woodland at Camberlot Road, **Lower Dicker**, Hellingly. The V1 exploded and completely wrecked a house on Camberlot Home Farm.

24 July. A raid on **Heathfield** at 3.05pm caused extensive damage to property. At 10.07pm 39 buildings were damaged at **Ewhurst**, and at 10.16pm property at **Buxted** suffered.

26 July. A flying bomb hit trees bordering the main Hastings road at **Windmill Hill** and exploded. There were 4 cottages at **Beacon Green** that were severely damaged and had to be demolished.

27 July. Just after midnight a V1 fell at **Ticehurst** and at 6.05am some 70 residences in **Polegate** were devastated. A further 54 homes were damaged when a V1 fell at **Buxted**.

28 July. Close to Ridgewood Farm, **Uckfield**, 27 houses were damaged by a flying bomb.

29 July. At Blackshaw, **Laughton**, damage to the vicarage was sustained. At 6.45pm 8 homes at Green Square in **Wadhurst** were rendered uninhabitable. At 11.08pm that night 3 buildings at **Ewhurst** were demolished and a dozen other buildings damaged.

30 July. It was the turn of **Newhaven**, as 34 homes in Gibbons Road, West Pier and South Road were damaged by a flying bomb. The V1 struck the cliffs at Newhaven Fort. (Near this spot, on 22 November that year, a British barge loaded with explosives broke away from its tug vessel in a storm and drifted ashore, striking a land mine at 5.00am. Its cargo of 180 tons of high explosive blew up, causing the largest explosion ever seen in the county.)

1 August. There were 40 houses at **Seddlescombe** damaged at 7.00am. At 9.05am a number of homes at **Nutley** sustained damage.

2 August. At 12.45pm the farmhouse and a pair of cottages at Moat House Farm, **Isfield**, suffered a bomb attack.

3 August. Dallingridge Farmhouse in **Forest Row** and 14 other buildings suffered V1 damage at 7.41am. An attack at 11.04am struck **Tidebrook** School near Wadhurst and demolished school property.

4 August. At 3.46am 20 homes at **East Grinstead** sustained bomb damage. At 3.58pm serious damage was caused to 4 **Battle** properties and slight damage to 118 others. Overall 374 V1 bombs were recorded in **Battle** Rural District and 166 habitable properties were destroyed. At 4.05pm a flying bomb struck near the Bell Inn at Shortgate, **Laughton**, wrecking the public house and 3 cottages opposite; 4 civilians died in this tragedy. The public house has since been rebuilt as The Bluebell.

5 August. A total of 10 homes at **Cross-in-Hand** and **Waldron** suffered a raid at 7.00am. At 4.35pm 50 homes at **Pevensey** were damaged and at 6.55pm a **Framfield** home was demolished.

6 August. Broomhill coastguard station look-out was slightly damaged and the rocket post wrecked at 4.42am.

7 August. Private residences around St Elisabeth's Church in **Eastbourne** were damaged around 11.16pm by a V1.

8 August. An 11.05pm attack at **Uckfield** claimed the post office at **Tintern Grange**; some 56 shops and homes were seriously damaged.

11 August. The final V1 reported in **Uckfield** district fell at Possingworth Park Hotel (again). It was extensively damaged and 20 houses were affected.

14 August. At 4.28am extensive damage was caused to **Rye** homes, buildings and a chemical works in Rye. The largest concentration of artillery in Britain was amassed between **Camber** and **Rye Harbour**, and 1,300 gunners manned the sites; 6 flying bombs were brought down in that district.

17 August. At Icklesham, **Rye Harbour**, at 6.13am extensive damage was caused to homes, a shop and a gun site. In the area 6 flying bombs were recorded.

18 August. At 7.05am in **Cuckfield** 4 homes were demolished and 3 were seriously damaged.

24 August. The last V1 to strike the Heathfield district fell at **Broad Oak**.

29 August. A V1 fatally struck the Officer's Mess at Marsh Green Army Camp near **Hartfield** at 1.52pm after an intercepting Spitfire had clipped the wing of the doodlebug, to turn it back towards the Channel. Casualties were taken to Queen Victoria Hospital, East Grinstead. A modest plaque, presented by men of no. 302 OCA 34th Regiment (QORWK) RATA no. 302 Battery, in Colemans Hatch church commemorates the tragedy. The commanding officer was said to be among those killed; 20 civilian properties were also damaged.

5 November. Extensive damage was inflicted on Frant Place at Calsey Wood, **Frant**, at 7.50pm.

13 November. A V2 rocket landed at 10.47pm at **Southborough**, Tunbridge Wells, creating a large crater. Luckily nobody was killed.

25 March 1945. The last reported V1 attack was at 7.58am in Lowdells Lane and Sackville Lane, **East Grinstead**; some 50 properties were damaged.

'*Forewarned is Forearmed*' was the proud motto of the Royal Observer Corps, which was founded in 1925 and served in various roles until the units were finally stood down on 30 September 1991. From the mid-1950s ROC duties changed from aircraft identification to the monitoring of nuclear bomb explosions and fall-out drift. Many of the now defunct ROC posts – there are around fifty of them across Sussex – are still evident. Although redundant, most of the bases have been sealed off, flooded or concealed with earthworks.

Top: an isolated 1940s surface ROC post on farmland at Magham Down. (*Gote House*). Middle: the county ROC No. 2 Group control centre was situated within MoD grounds at Denne Road, Horsham. Recollections of their activities are best seen in the reconstructions at Newhaven Fort. An exterior post is seen in the second view. (*Gote House*). Bottom left: the interior of a Cold War period bunker, at the site of the first photograph. It gives an idea of the bunker's modest size – 15 ft x 7½ ft. These bunkers could accommodate three staff. Most of the ROC posts of this type were built between 1958 and 1965. (*Gote House*). Bottom right: the air-tight cantilever access hatch of an underground post, near Fletching. The monitoring room below is now flooded. (*Gote House*)

REPLICA OF A WW2 OBSERVER CORPS POST WITH THE INSTRUMENT USED FOR PLOTTING AIRCRAFT IN FLIGHT.

REUNION.

DAY JUNE 19ᵗʰ

00 to 1800

(MEETING 1400)

NEWHAVEN FORT

THE HOME OF

The most exclusive Second World War bunkers were those created for the Auxiliary Units patrols of the Home Guard No. 203 volunteers. The twenty-five Sussex patrols each consisted of about six men, all trained in deadly rearguard sabotage operations. A full account of the Sussex Auxiliary Units has been recorded in *Secret Sussex Resistance* by Stewart Angell. (*Gote House*)

The exclusive badge of the Home Guard GHQ (Reserve) Battalions No. 201, 202 and 203. (*Bill Webber*)

The author and Stewart Angell discovered and excavated the entrance to the lost hide-out of the Hellingly patrol in mid-1998. (*Gote House*)

A view into a typical abandoned Auxiliary Units retreat, complete with bunk beds and escape tunnel entrance. This was the Staplefield patrol base. (*Stewart Angell*)

THE WILDERNESS, BROADWATER DOWN, TUNBRIDGE WELLS

Several tales concerning the Second World War occupation of the bunker beneath Hargate Forest are linked to Field Marshal Montgomery. In fact, he has been quoted as saying that he knew nothing whatsoever of this bunker and never used headquarters bunkers himself as they were, in his view, bad for troop morale. He is said to have arrived in Tunbridge Wells on 12 April 1941 and when he was promoted he moved to a new HQ at Reigate on 17 November 1941.

The Broadwater Down bunker is not thought to have ever been occupied, despite the extensive tunnels. A former member of the Royal Engineers no. 172 Tunnelling Company has stated that they started to dig tunnels at The Wilderness in 1940 and it took them about a year to complete. They blasted their way initially, but ran into several problems. As well as misfires they had to cope with the perils of rock falls and flooding. They worked in three shifts of eight hours, and blasting took place during daylight hours. The job was finished in late 1941 and the company left for Gibraltar in early 1942.

A workman who had fitted power cables revisited the tunnels in 1946 to retrieve cabling. He reckoned that the bunker had never been used, as it was devoid of any equipment, heating or lighting. The bunker was at that time in good condition, with no water seepage evident. In the late 1960s a local builder and two colleagues explored the then flooded tunnelling with a dinghy, but they could only travel a short distance as they found water up to the roof.

The plan shown here was initiated by diving club members during the drought of May 1976, and work continued late in 1979. One of their members contacted over a dozen official MoD sources, local authorities and record offices, endeavouring to find out more about the tunnels – to no avail. Given recent housing development above ground and lack of tunnel maintenance, formal knowledge of this bunker must be deemed as lost with the passage of time.

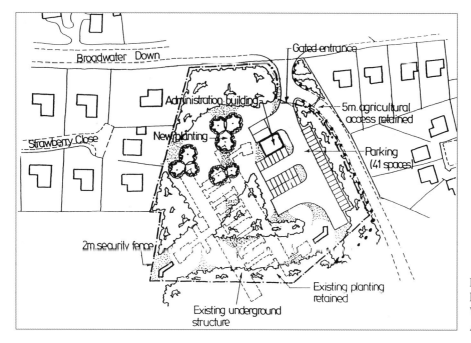

Broadwater Down, Tunbridge Wells. (*Via BC Archive – adapted*)

St Clement's Caves, Hastings. These caverns date back centuries and have been used by both civilians and military personnel. In the 1940s they were adopted by ARP officials as shelters for up to 600 civilians. (*Gote House*)

St Clement's Caves, Hastings

A popular tourist attraction has been established at St Clement's Caves at Hastings. The caverns were used for smuggling in the eighteenth century and in the Napoleonic Wars they were converted into hospital facilities for soldiers under the Duke of Wellington. Access was later sealed off by owner Edward Millward, owing to intrusions and vandalism.

In 1825 a gardener working above the caves accidentally dug through the rock and rediscovered the complex of caves. Subsequently the caverns have been used for various purposes. During the Second World War they were adapted as ARP shelters for up to 600 people, including some made homeless by the bombing. Sandy flooring was concreted over to make the place more habitable. A bomb struck the nearby cliffs, although the caves were not affected. Official town records were stored in the caves, but they had to be moved when dampness caused problems.

D-Day Command Centre, Wentworth

Although this book focuses on Sussex I make no excuse for including locations on the county borders like this interesting bunker under a luxurious private estate between Sunningdale and Virginia Water in Surrey. The famous world-class golf course is the best-known feature of the estate and Wentworth House was adapted as the clubhouse.

Wentworth bunker is described by Peter Laurie in *Beneath the City Streets* as one of several alternative D-Day bunkers. The bunker lies to the south of Wentworth House and

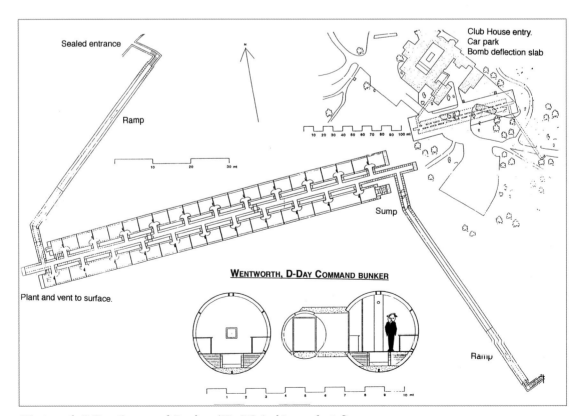

Wentworth D-Day Command Bunker. (*Via BC Archive – adapted*)

consists of segmented parallel cast-iron tubes, supposedly as used on the London Underground. Each section is about 330 ft in length. The tubes are divided by a narrow access tunnel and via ramps and stairways from the clubhouse entry point. A thick concrete slab, later used as a car park, was laid to make the bunker bomb-proof, with ventilation shafts at intervals.

PRO documents indicate that the Wentworth bunker was devised for use as headquarters if London was flattened by extensive bombing raids and if mass evacuation of the capital was necessary. In 1941 the bunker was designated for use by General Sir Alan Brooke, C.-in-C. Home Forces, as an invasion HQ. However, it became a signals centre for the 21st Army Group in the build-up to D-Day.

When it was visited in the 1970s, the bunker was said to be in sound condition still, although all cables and suspended flooring had been removed.

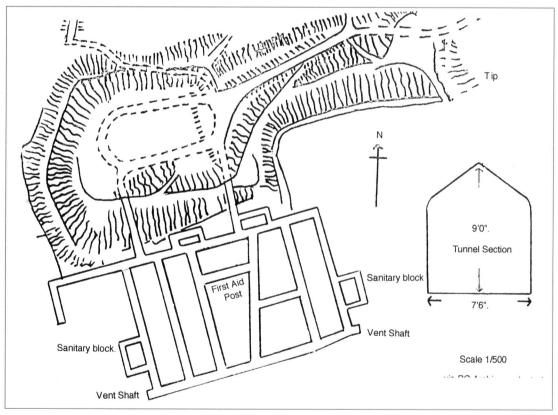

Foxenden Quarry Shelter, Guildford. (*Via BC Archive – adapted*)

FOXENDEN QUARRY SHELTER, GUILDFORD

Unlike some Second World War bunkers and ARP shelters in the south-east, where MoD sources and County Record Offices often deny any knowledge of the sites, this retreat was comparatively well recorded and access was possible via local council offices. Surrey Record Office's Minutes of the Emergency Committee of Guildford Borough Council refers to this shelter.

On 11 November 1940 the Emergency Committee called for the Borough Surveyor to devise a plan for a deep shelter to accommodate 1,000 civilians. In time this figure was increased to 2,500 people and it was decided that there was no need to line the chalk walling. The plans went as far as ambitiously suggesting that after the war the tunnel could be developed into an underground highway to alleviate town traffic congestion.

A tender for a trial section of tunnel was accepted on 22 November 1940. Then on 7 February 1941 the full contract was assigned to Messrs J.B. Edwards & Co. (Whyteleafe) Ltd and was to be completed in six or seven weeks.

On 23 March 1941 the developers stated that their work would not be completed in time and applied to Surrey County Council for an extension to the schedule. In fact the tunnelling was completed by the end of September 1941. Final payment was made in mid-December that year. The complete cost of the work was £5,500. Towards the end of the war the tunnels were not occupied, nor were they used for storage, and after the war they were finally sealed off.

DEEPDENE HOUSE, DORKING

Similar tunnelling layouts were used in various bunkers shown in this book. In 1939 Deepdene House, Dorking, was occupied by Southern Railway officials for use as an emergency HQ control centre should the evacuation of London take place.

Deepdene House has since been demolished and modern office units erected. The railway people made the tunnels into an underground telephone exchange. The tunnels were said to pre-date the war, but were enlarged considerably as shelters and stores.

A pair of long tunnels run in parallel, with cross-over tubes. The walls were lined with concrete or corrugated iron. Railway track was used for roof support and protection. A 52-ft escape shaft rose to a bricked outlet camouflaged by fencing. The tunnel known as East Cave was about 85 ft long. The last section was lined with natural sandstone, and an escape route in the domed roof admitted daylight. These tunnels are now sealed off and rendered inaccessible as they are in a dangerous condition.

Plan of Deepdene House, Dorking. Additional premises were acquired at Elmstead Woods in Kent and a section of Brighton Locomotive Works was requisitioned as emergency control units. (*Via BC Archive – adapted*)

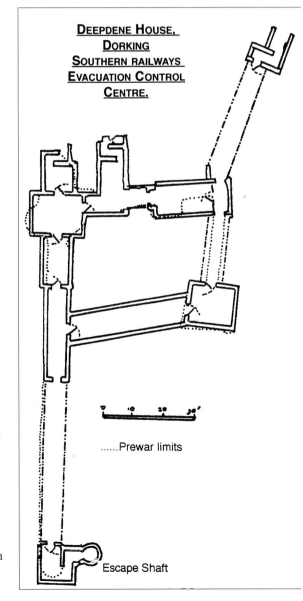

DEEPDENE HOUSE, DORKING SOUTHERN RAILWAYS EVACUATION CONTROL CENTRE.

......Prewar limits

Escape Shaft

Below the Guinness Trust Home at South Heighton troops of No. 2 Section 172 Tunnelling Company of Royal Engineers excavated the honeycomb of Royal Navy communications tunnels that became HMS *Forward* in 1941. See page 49. (*Gote House*)

An exhaustive record of the construction and occupation of the South Heighton tunnels has been published in book and video format by Geoffrey Ellis as *The Secret Tunnels of South Heighton*. Local research groups are making plans to enable the western exit section of the tunnel to be opened for public appraisal. A scale model of HMS *Forward* is on view in Newhaven Local & Maritime History Museum in Avis Road, Denton. (*Gote House*)

A pair of observation post tunnels were cut by Royal Engineers at Newhaven Fort out towards the cliff face. The opening is currently concealed by a rock fall. The square holes seen in the cliff face were cut during the construction of the fort in the 1860s to support a steam hoist that lifted shingle for building work. The 1940s tunnel at Newhaven Fort is divided into two, but it has now caved in. It was constructed using steel loop support sections and galvanised corrugated-iron sheet lining similar to those deployed at HMS *Forward* nearby. (*Gote House*)

Urban development over the fifty years since the war has swept away the majority of ARP shelters that were hurriedly created in residential areas. In the 1950s it was commonplace for school playgrounds and sports fields to feature sealed-up or grassed-over entry points to emergency dug-outs. (*Gote House*)

Top: these ARP shelters in Lewes are now adapted for grounds maintenance equipment. (*Gote House*). Middle and bottom: at Malling and the Pells these sealed-off shelters are typically associated with often exaggerated tales of their occupation. (*Gote House*)

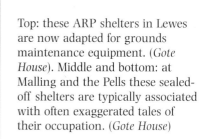

Morrison shelters were named after Herbert Morrison, Home Secretary in Churchill's Coalition government. These iron and steel shelters were allocated to homes to protect occupants during air-raids. Families often slept under the shelter, or used the top as a table. (*Gote House*)

Morrison shelters are still to be seen in the countryside. This one was used by the farmer to hold produce and milk churns waiting for roadside collection. (*Gote House*)

Sir John Anderson, also a member of the War Cabinet, gave his name to the corrugated-iron Anderson shelters issued to homes. Sir John, later Lord Waverley, lived at West Dean in Friston Forest and is buried at All Saints' Church in the hamlet. After the war countless Anderson shelters found new uses as garden or allotment sheds. (*Gote House*)

VISCOUNT WAVERLEY
1882 — 1958

John Anderson, first Viscount Waverley of Westdean, Knight Grand Cross of the Bath, Member of the Order of Merit, Knight Grand Commander of the Star of India, Knight Grand Commander of the Indian Empire, one of her Majesty's Most Honourable Privy Council and a Fellow of the Royal Society, Governor of Bengal, Member of Parliament for the Scottish Universities, Lord Privy Seal, Home Secretary, Lord President of the Council, Chancellor of the Exchequer, a Member of the War Cabinet, Chairman of the Port of London Authority.

Pillboxes survive in curious locations. This example guards the staggered sections of the Royal Military Canal near Rye. (*Gote House*)

A cluster of decaying pillboxes can be found at Barcombe Mills, near Lewes, in the meadows alongside the River Ouse. (*Gote House*)

Marked on Ashdown Forest maps as 'The Old Airstrip', the wartime heathland clearing is known to present-day pilots of light aircraft as an emergency landing ground. (*Gote House*)

ASHDOWN FOREST AIRSTRIP

Information about the creation of the 1940s airstrip has been gleaned via contributors to past editions of the *Ashdown Forest News*. A chance meeting in Canada during a mid-1990s holiday led to one correspondent meeting a former Canadian Army captain named Douglas Van Kleek, who has since passed away. In mid-1943 Van Kleek was serving with the First Canadian Mechanical Equipment Company. He was instructed to set up a school to teach British Army officers and service NCOs, in groups of six to eight, to operate and use heavy mechanical equipment such as shovels, graders and bulldozers.

This training later enabled them to construct temporary anti-aircraft gun emplacements and improvised landing strips in Europe. Each course lasted about two weeks and consisted of 25 per cent lectures and 75 per cent operations. The gun emplacements were levelled after each class, but the landing strip was extended class by class. Van Kleek's recollection was that there was a cluster of buildings near the main A22 highway, originally used by cyclists and hikers, which the Army duly adopted for accommodation and mess rooms. By early July 1943 the British Army had taken over and added more huts, and the Canadians went under canvas until they moved to Italy in September. At this time the earthwork project ended.

Thus was the heathland emergency landing ground established. It served its purpose during the early afternoon of Monday 6 September 1943. Over forty USAAF B-17 bombers, low on fuel and simply lost, straggled back across the Sussex coast. They had been called back from a raid on Stuttgart when a fighter escort failed to materialise and by midday the crews were exhausted. At least one of these bombers came down on the Ashdown Forest runway.

Local eye-witnesses still talk of the occasion when one B-17 attempted to take off again from the makeshift airstrip. After several unsuccessful attempts to lift off the rescue crew of the mighty Flying Fortress jettisoned all surplus equipment and lashed the aircraft to a tree beside the A22. The engines were fired up to maximum power, then the moorings were broken and the B-17 roared down the airstrip and finally took off, heading back towards its East Anglian aerodrome.

ROEDEAN SCHOOL – HMS *VERNON*

The notion that the nation's most prestigious girls' school can also boast an Old Boys group of former seamen may sound bizarre – but it is none the less true! On 7 April 1951 Roedean Girls' School became the barracks and training quarters called HMS *Vernon*. Situated on cliff-top pastures alongside the A259 between Brighton and Rottingdean the robust neo-Baroque school looks out over the English Channel. In 1994, some fifty years after his time at Roedean, Sam Morley enquired at the school if a group of septuagenarian ex-sailors could visit the premises again. Roedean staff were more than pleased to hear from the former sailor and on 20 July 1994 some fifty-four ex-seamen were reunited at the school and the Roedean Old Boys' Association was created.

The famous school originated amid the splendour of the mid-Victorian era when three sisters, Dorothy, Penelope and Millicent Lawrence, purchased a house in Lewes Crescent, Kemp Town, Brighton. They called their home Wimbledon House, after their previous home, and soon opened a school there. It flourished and they were able to buy the present site in 1895. The new school opened its doors to the first pupils in 1899.

An airman's view of Roedean School – HMS *Vernon*. Fortunately the school was never seriously attacked. (*Roedean School Archives*)

Roedean School closed in mid-1940 and staff and pupils were evacuated to the comparative safety of Keswick in the Lake District. A contingent of Argyll Sutherland Highlanders moved in to the school immediately for training and they occupied no. 3 building. They were followed by the Queens Royal Regiment and then a quartet of Canadian regiments and London Scottish troops. The Royal Navy next took command of the premises after its Portsmouth submariners' headquarters had been bombed heavily. While the White Ensign flew from the flagstaff of Roedean's quadrangle – renamed the Quarter Deck – 31,500 HMS *Vernon* officers and men passed through Roedean on various courses covering torpedoes, ship's electrics, mines, navigation, coding and depth-charges.

Countless tales from that time circulate. Beneath a bell push above each student's bed at Roedean was an ivorine label engraved with the words 'Press the button if you need a mistress for any reason during the night.' Optimistic young sailors soon found that any such summons brought instead an irate petty officer! When the Royal Navy first occupied the school there were still a few sixth formers there. The HMS *Vernon* CO, so the story goes, insisted that the young ladies move out before the sailors arrived. The prim school mistress in charge responded: 'My girls will be all right, they've got it up there' – tapping her forehead. The CO supposedly replied: 'Madam, it matters not where your girls have got it, rest assured my sailors will find it.'

LANCING COLLEGE – HMS *KING ALFRED*

In mid-1940 Lancing College was requisitioned as an officers' training school, as part of the HMS *King Alfred* unit on Hove seafront. During four years of naval occupation the

The imposing chapel at Lancing College dominates the countryside. (*Gote House*)

imposing Gothic college saw huge numbers of men training to be officers; indeed their numbers far exceeded the number of pupils passing through the school since its founding in 1848 by Nathaniel Woodard. A bust of General Sir Bernard Montgomery records his time at Lancing College in the early 1940s.

In the week after Dunkirk the college masters at Lancing College seriously considered evacuation away from the coastal plain. Brother colleges at Denstone in Staffordshire and Ellesmere in Shropshire agreed to take the Lancing personnel and evacuation began on 27 June 1940. During their last week in Sussex the pupils and staff endured two air-raids, each lasting for some five hours. Staff put their furniture into store on the morning of 27 June, but troops soon began taking it all out again. Nearby soldiers were demolishing the shanty town development on Shoreham Beach, to provide a clear field of fire out to sea. This also provided a valuable supply of timber for shoring up buildings in emergencies.

The British Third Division was stationed nearby at Brighton and received priority in re-equipping – it had been about to sail for France when resistance there collapsed. When the Army moved out of the college, after some months, the buildings were adopted by the Admiralty and became HMS *King Alfred*, along with the requisitioned King Alfred sports complex on Hove seafront.

A total of 1,150 Old Lancing pupils served in the Armed Services in the Second World War. They won 103 decorations, and 23 ex-pupils were Mentioned in Despatches. Sadly, 137 lost their lives – almost half of those killed were serving in the RAF. Over the winter of 1944/5 the Admiralty began to cut down the HMS *King Alfred* network and the Lancing complex was de-requisitioned by mid-1945.

Despite its landmark location at the foot of the Downs, overlooking Shoreham airfield, the vulnerable college and its mammoth chapel were never a serious target for enemy aircraft and the majestic buildings survived the war virtually unscathed.

RAF DURRINGTON RADAR STATION

A great deal of mystery surrounds wartime, and indeed postwar, activity around the former mansion at Field Place, Worthing, and the former RAF Durrington Ground Control Interception (GCI) radar station. This was the first of the original six GCI stations and was established on the outskirts of Worthing in 1941. Pre-war plans for residential development of the area provided a useful network of roads, although the houses themselves had yet to be built. Initial trials with a mobile GCI unit involved aerial arrays and other equipment mounted on the back of RAF trucks trundling across the fields around Durrington.

This work was replaced by an Intermediate hutted station and later by the final GCI 'Happidrome' operations block from 1942. Administration for the complex was based nearby at Field Place, which served as a domestic site (barracks) for staff. WAAFs were billeted in nearby houses. In 1953 the 'Happidrome' (named after a popular wartime radio programme) was converted for use as the main building of Palatine School, by simply painting over the austere brickwork and altering windows and some internal walls.

On 21 July 2000 commemoration of the founding of the first GCI unit at Durrington was held. Plaques were presented at Palatine School and Field Place, with former Armed Services personnel in attendance. Intrigue abounds at these sites but an embargo prevents

Field Place, Worthing, housed the RAF Durrington GCI radar station from 1941. A great deal of intrigue still surrounds the building and its wartime role, as files about it at the PRO remain closed. (*Gote House*)

Palatine Special Needs School, Worthing, has made good use of the former RAF 'Happidrome' operations block since it was de-requisitioned in 1953. Originally built in 1941, the block was camouflaged by the RAF with timber and sheeting to resemble a remote farm barn. (*Gote House*)

The main hall at St James Primary School, Chichester, was requisitioned as RAF Tangmere's distant Sector A operations centre, after the devastating attacks of mid-August 1940. (*Gote House*)

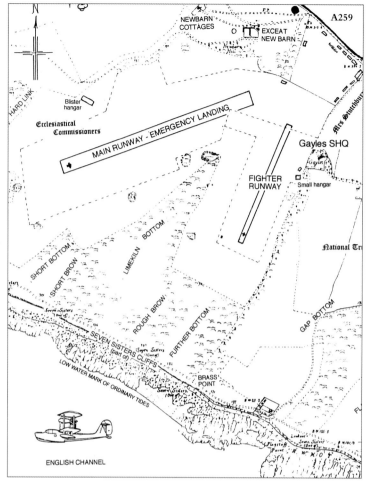

Map showing RAF Friston aerodrome. The wartime Sussex airfields were commemorated in the run-up to the new millennium. Gatherings took place in the mid-1990s at various former advanced landing grounds; the defunct RAF stations at Coolham, Deanland and Chailey all received due attention. In April 2001 RAF Friston aerodrome was remembered. The Royal Society of St George, together with local church officials, organised a reunion and a service of remembrance. (*Gote House*)

This image of a lady singing reflects the fact that BBC radio programmes became bastions of morale and communications. (*Gote House*)

access to relevant PRO files. Local people, especially those who were children at the time, tell vivid tales of exploring tunnels that ran from Field Place out to Durrington GCI. There is talk of some 6 miles of tunnels, containing surplus steel tables, old bicycles, redundant fire-extinguishers and light fittings, and of 500 Harley-Davidson motor-cycles stored there before D-Day. Tunnels supposedly stretched from the children's play area at West Park to Field Place and on via Durrington station to The Strand where a military hospital was created. The Inland Revenue's Barrington Road offices now occupy the site of the hospital. Tunnels also ran, it is said, to the GCI station itself in Palatine School. Reportedly the main operations room, some 20 ft under Field Place's ancient putting ground, was 23 ft wide and about 40 ft long.

Preliminary exploration has revealed water tanks, a well and ventilation shafts, as well as the main transport entrance and pillars. Access to the tunnel is said to be through rooms in Field Place or via a ventilation shaft in front of the building – these entry points have been sealed off or concealed.

Numerous other school premises were requisitioned during the Second World War. The school hall at St James Primary School in St James Road, Chichester, became the Sector A operations centre after the decisive enemy attack on RAF Tangmere on 16 August 1940, thus creating a proud heritage for the pupils of later years.

Subsequently a hall at Bishop Otter College in Chichester was commandeered as the D-Day Operations Centre from 15 February 1944. Here an observation gallery was erected above, where staff managed a pair of plotting tables, personnel, desks, telephones and huge boards showing aerial activity. From January to May 1945 the premises were maintained as an Emergency Operations room with nominal staff.

One of my earliest memories relates to Balfour Road School in Brighton in about 1950, when I was five years old. The school had been held in reserve as an emergency hospital during the war. I can recall wondering why a door in Miss Bishop's class-room had the word KITCHEN painted in black on its heavily varnished surface. . . .

THE WIRELESS YEARS

The general regard for radio broadcasting had risen greatly in the 1930s. Amid the pressures of the early 1940s the BBC was to be a great stalwart that duly enhanced society and advanced with the technical progression of warfare. Many people came to rely heavily on their radio sets.

Interest in Britain's military past can take many forms. Collecting official and civilian 1940s propaganda and information sheets and posters, like those seen here, offers a low-cost pastime of considerable interest. (*Gote House*)

Dame Vera Lynn has long been associated with Sussex. In the early 1940s she lived with her musician husband Vic Lewis under the Downs at Underhill Lane, Clayton, north of Brighton. In more recent years Dame Vera has been a well-known resident of Ditchling. Miss Anne Shelton was another popular singer of that time who had a house in Sussex.

Radio celebrities became national figures, and many programmes became immensely popular, reaching vast audiences. Henry Hall, Jack Payne, Sandy MacPherson, Wilfrid Pickles, Christopher Stone, Tommy Handley, Dorothy Summers, Jack Train, Arthur Askey, Richard Murdoch, Gracie Fields, Bebe Daniels and Ben Lyon are but a few of the hallowed radio stars of the wartime period. Many of these personalities lived in Sussex.

Tottington Barn is now used by the Youth Hostel Association as a hostel on the South Downs Way at Truleigh Hill, Shoreham. It was built in the 1930s in the centre of a naturists' colony. Sun worshippers would laze on the balcony in front of the remote property. More recently the balcony has been built over.

During the 1940s the building was requisitioned by the RAF, who had established nearby an intermediate Chain Home Low radar station with sets of masts. PRO files state that as at 26 April 1942 an officer and twenty-two other ranks guarded the Truleigh Hill AMES site. The Air Ministry had metalled the Mill Hill by-way from Erringham Farm to service the radar station and afford access to the army training ranges, that took over numerous farms and vast areas of downland.

A similar steep tank road from Castle Town, Upper Beeding, off the A2037, to the radar station is less well maintained and is now deeply rutted. (*Gote House*)

On Friday 22 May 1942 the Spitfire of Sergeant Pilot H.E. Barton crashed into the end of Stamford Buildings – the former Firle Workhouse – on the old A27 highway east of Lewes. The pilot sadly died in the accident and twenty-five people were evacuated when much of the property was demolished. (*Gote House*)

'Dragon's Teeth' anti-invasion blocks are still to be found at numerous Sussex locations. This neat row of bollards was re-positioned after the war to prevent motorists driving on to Alfriston's communal recreation ground. During the war these anti-tank blocks were officially called pimples in quaint War Ministry parlance. (*Gote House*)

Another roadside show of 'Dragon's Teeth' near Stonegate station, Burwash. (*Gote House*)

These 'Dragon's Teeth' now line a junction leading to a small estate at Ditchling. (*Gote House*)

These re-positioned anti-tank bollards have lined a car park in Lewes for many years now. (*Gote House*)

Visitors to Pevensey Castle are often confused by the profusion of Second World War pillboxes and gun posts preserved at this historic site, now managed by English Heritage. The castle grounds were occupied at various times by American, Canadian and British troops. The crumbling stone walls were used to conceal the observation and gun positions. Today these are retained, with some entrances sealed off. Gaping embrasures, however, are witness to their defensive role in the 1940s. (*Gote House*)

A number of mobile target tank ranges near the coast have been investigated. Residents and former servicemen recall 2-ft narrow-gauge railway lines re-sited at Belle Tout, near Beachy Head, and at Balsdean Farm near Rottingdean. Another track ran for about a mile from the back of South Hill Barn (above) to the Seven Sisters cliff edge on Seaford Head.

The South Hill track carried three or four bogies in a 4-ft-deep trench. The chassis carried a mock-up of a tank for gunnery practice. Former staff of B. Berry & Sons' forge in Seaford recall that the tank target was often sent to them for straightening out! (*Gote House*)

Aircraft-related artefacts are still being found in Sussex. In April 2000 Paul Foulkcs-Halbard found three rusting rockets embedded in the base of a tree bordering his Filching Manor estate near Eastbourne. Two of the rockets have since been removed. They are thought to have come from the Tempest Sabre IIA fighter in which Flight Sergeant Roland Wright from New Zealand fatally crashed while trying to intercept a doodlebug on 28 July 1944. (*Gote House*)

1940s street life . . . youngsters collect metal salvage for recycling. A home from home often developed as a result of the continuous occupation of civilian shelters. (*Newhaven Fort*)

1940s street life . . . the removal of iron railings and gates for munitions has left a curious legacy of sawn-off iron stubs on many Sussex walls. (*Newhaven Fort*)

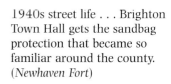

1940s street life . . . Brighton Town Hall gets the sandbag protection that became so familiar around the county. (*Newhaven Fort*)

4

The Cold War & Beyond

Firemen lay lighting cables during a 1988 inspection of the redundant RAF radar
bunker at Beachy Head, which was constructed by George Wimpey & Co. between
1949 and 1953. The Air Ministry had finally relinquished the Cold War bunker in
1961. Auctioneers Geering & Colyer held a sale of operating equipment on site on
23 April 1963, after plans for a Civil Defence facility failed. In 1989 developments
for a museum and visitor centre in the bunker were curtailed. Entrance to the
underground passages was sealed off in late 1995 during a downland conservation
programme. (*T.R. Beckett Ltd*)

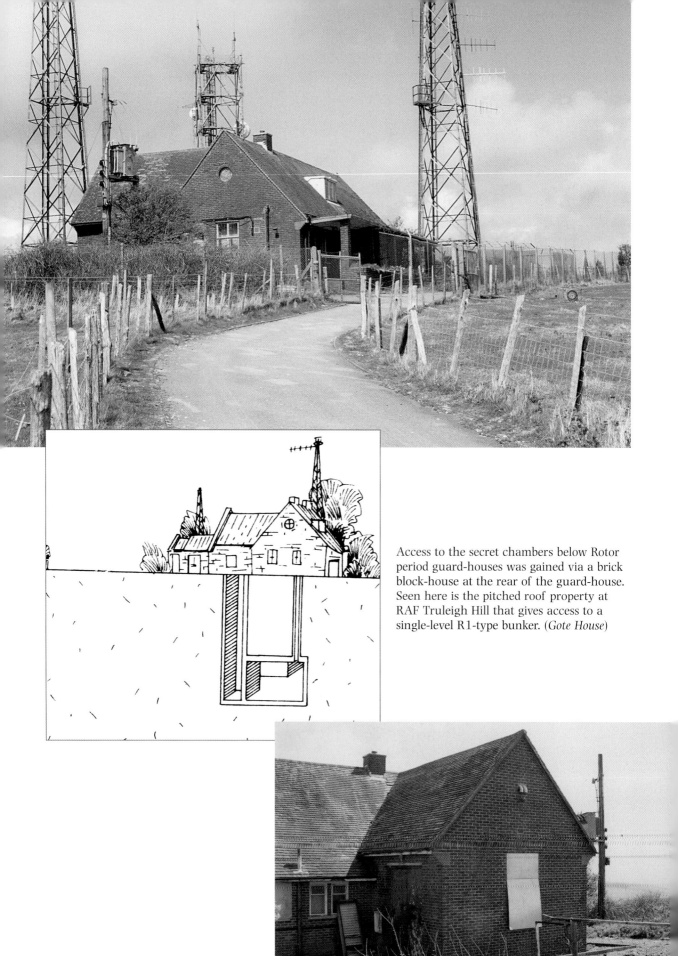

Access to the secret chambers below Rotor period guard-houses was gained via a brick block-house at the rear of the guard-house. Seen here is the pitched roof property at RAF Truleigh Hill that gives access to a single-level R1-type bunker. (*Gote House*)

The term Cold War is defined as the use of propaganda, obstruction, intimidation and subversive political activities to secure an advantage. The years after the Second World War witnessed a new type of hostility in international relations. At the centre of the Cold War between Russia and the Allies was the divided city of Berlin, with the famous airlift, Operation Vittles, of June 1948 to September 1949 and the infamous Berlin Wall.

In the UK the economic and diplomatic offensive was supported by a rapidly developed schedule of defensive measures, of which airborne resources and radar systems assumed priority. The jet age was crucial for the government, backed up with the commercial potential for civilian flight, manufacturing and export. While the Cold War programme engulfed its seemingly limitless budget, with equipment and property often being almost obsolete by the time it became operational, much of the activity was conducted in secrecy, presenting an intriguing legacy for archivists and the public.

At a number of administrative centres such as county halls and civic blocks, Cold War emergency retreats were created, often as an extension of the 1940s ARP bunkers. Emergency planning exercises for public services were carried out under various guises across the country – and still are. It is for such purposes that numerous Cold War bunkers have been re-equipped, even if only in a nominal role as resources become restricted or outmoded. Major flooding, transport incidents or hospital needs can all be managed from these civic bunkers.

EMERGENCY ADMINISTRATIVE CENTRES

The main Cold War bunker in Sussex was created at Kings Standing, near Crowborough, by developing the 1940s site built for the Operation Aspidistra black propaganda programme. This covert wartime base intercepted domestic German wavelengths in contravention of the Geneva Convention. It was highly successful.

Described as a Wireless Telegraph Station for the Diplomatic Service the redundant Kings Standing complex was eventually modernised at colossal cost to become one of fourteen regional centres in Britain. Up to 200 key personnel would be accommodated, ready to assume control of essential services in the aftermath of a nuclear attack. Today the bunker's confines are occupied by the Sussex Police Authority as a training facility, but the future of the maze of redundant buildings is in doubt as the air-conditioning plant and generators become increasingly costly to maintain or replace. The Foreign & Commonwealth Office put the site and its structures up for sale by public auction in May 1986. Scrap contractors stripped out the old surplus machinery. Local newspapers reported the site as being on the market for £300,000, but the sale was halted and the Sussex Police Authority took over the Ashdown Forest compound.

Under the 1984 County War Emergency Plan East Sussex was in Sub-region 61, organised from the control room under County Hall in Lewes.

REGIONAL SEATS OF GOVERNMENT

The three-storey Cold War bunker at Kelvedon Hatch in Essex has been resurrected as a tourist and educational facility and has been kitted out with period office equipment, supplies and uniformed mannequins, etc. The bunker had been advertised for sale by sealed public tender with a guide price of just £150,000, although that figure was well short of the price it eventually realised. There were twenty bidders for the cavernous retreat. It was bought by farmer Mike Parrish of Pump House Farm; this was not inappropriate as the bunker had been excavated 100 ft below the Essex countryside that his family had farmed for five generations.

The MoD moved out in 1994 and the Parrish family set about their new task. The former Cold War bunker was first opened to the public in January 1995 and over a hundred people came to view the complex.

The modest entry point to the nuclear retreat at the Brede Water Works compound in East Sussex. Note the two air vents. This shelter was commissioned as late as December 1992. The building was erected, as directed by the Secretary of State for the Environment, to ensure that the company met the requirements of Section 20B of the Water Industry Act 1991 to provide a secure control centre for the water industry in the event of war. (*Gote House*)

It seems likely that other public services had similar facilities. The building at Brede is said to be a Tom Butler Mk 4 design. Many period office blocks have such units. Various clues are to be found in such buildings: exhaust cowling in roofs, air infiltration hoods on outer walls, and an inlet into the wall for foam control. They were built to the latest specifications, with twin generators, full positive air management systems with manual back-up, and dormitory units for staff sleeping on a shift basis. Later blocks took fifty people for two or three months' occupation. The interior air-tight chamber (seen on the left), with 14-in-thick walls, is screened off from the initial wash-down unit at the Brede surface shelter. (*Gote House*)

POSTWAR BUNKERS AND SHELTERS

Given the intensity of the Cold War threat at one time, it is hardly surprising that front-line Sussex retains a number of subterranean curios in the form of military and civil retreats. The most obvious of the clandestine administrative units are the 1950s Rotor period RAF radar stations, now devoid of equipment and invariably derelict, sealed off or flooded. Obsolete Royal Observer Corps posts, from the forty-five sites dispersed across Sussex, are similarly in various stages of decay.

RAF Rye Chain Home radar station retains several abandoned surface buildings dating from the 1940s. Postwar radar bunkers at Beachy Head and Fairlight have been decommissioned, grassed over and sealed off. Operations at RAF Pevensey CH and RAF Wartling GCI stations finally ended in 1964 and the land is now primarily agricultural again. Various masts at RAF Truleigh Hill CHL, which now facilitate contemporary communications systems, cluster around the typical 1950s RAF guard-house above the single-level R1 bunker, reportedly now let out for storage.

Perhaps an unexpected addition to the list of official retreats is the air-tight surface shelter created in the early 1990s within the Southern Water Authority compound at Brede Water Works, off the A28 opposite the Red Lion Inn, 6 miles north of Hastings. Planning for the single-level Brede shelter, situated on a former staff car park, must have begun in the late 1980s at a time when the fourteen national Regional Seat of Government (RSG) centres were already being declared redundant and put out to tender. The Brede shelter was built to house up to fifty key personnel designated to manage the utility services in case of regional emergency. They could be secreted away for three months and were entirely self-sufficient within their confines, under a 12-in-thick double reinforced roof. There were bunks for around two dozen people, in three dormitories, and sleeping would have been on a shift basis. A similarly modest kitchen and small dining area supported the shift pattern.

Inside the Brede shelter were a pair of administration rooms designed to service staff needs. One room featured the escape hatch. In an adjoining room a ray-proof EMP (Electro Magnetic Pulse) unit called a Faraday Cage could maintain communications in an emergency. The shielding system would have a radio-telephone link to the outside world. Initial entry to the Brede shelter includes a nominal shower block to wash away contamination, prior to entry to an air-lock chamber, taking three or four people. Foul air would be allowed to escape by way of circular Andair discs set in the 14-in-thick walls. To the left is the toilet and washroom sector, with a number of water storage tanks. Beyond the dining and kitchen area, dormitories and administration rooms led to the Faraday Cage. The corridor leads on to the air-intake plant, which filtered incoming air for the occupants. In the next room was the industrial diesel engine that kept the shelter independent of outside sources, although for Open Days a 100-amp, 3-phase mains supply is utilised. Beyond this access returns to the air-lock and entry point.

Although devoid of furnishings and communications equipment the air-tight shelter is maintained ready for occupation by civilian utility service personnel, in case of regional emergency. The shelter was first opened to the public when Brede Steam Engine Society staged its annual Open Day in May 2000. The splendidly recreated pumping station is open to the public every first Saturday of the month, and the Grade II Listed pump-house, in magnificent Baroque and Art Deco styles, is well worth visiting.

The equipment at Brede includes this EMP Faraday Cage where an underground radio/telephone operator could maintain communication with the outside world. (*Gote House*)

Some low-budget shelters were sealed by back-filling the air-tight hatch at the main entrance with earth, so that entry to the bunker was by the escape hatch only. However, this hatch, in the main control room at Brede, was purely a means of escape. (*Gote House*)

The control shelter at Brede is still maintained ready for occupation at 48 hours notice in case of regional emergency. (*Gote House*)

Sleeping and dining areas could accommodate only part of the staff at any one time and a shift system would have been in use. (*Gote House*)

The crucial clean air filtration plant, nuclear screening and self-contained diesel generator plant ensures the bunker's independence from the outside world. (*Gote House*)

By Order of the Secretary of State for Air

DEMOLITION SALES

at the two

OLD R.A.F. TECHNICAL SITES

Nr. RYE and PEVENSEY, SUSSEX

Brick, Sectional Timber and Handcraft Buildings
6 350ft. Steel Towers
2 Water Towers

AND THE CONTENTS OF THE BUILDINGS

including

2 Mirrlees 102 h.p. Deisel Engines, Electrical Equipment and All Fittings, Steel and Timber Doors and Windows. Air Ventilation Systems, Fuel and Water Tanks, Sewage Pumps, Electric Motors, Tubular Wall Heaters, R.S.J.'s, Baths and Sinks

Power Cable

and other Miscellaneous Items

which

Messrs. James

WOODHAMS & SON

have been instructed to offer for Sale by Auction

On the Sites

on

WEDNESDAY & THURSDAY, 12th & 13th NOV., 1958

Sales commence at 2 p.m.

On view day prior to Sale from 10 a.m. to 4 p.m. and morning of Sale from 9.30 a.m.

Auction Offices — 27 High Street, Battle, Sussex. Tel. 37 and 449.

Barrett of Battle Ltd., Printers. 77 High Street (Tel. : 212).

Just another auctioneer's catalogue brings to an end twenty years of toil and endeavour for RAF and WAAF personnel. (*Gote House*)

The old plotting table in the main operations room at RAF Wartling, GCI station. The 1960s witnessed the end of an illustrious era, as the former RAF radar stations across Sussex were declared redundant. Once-bustling corridors and operations rooms have become derelict and dangerous since contractors stripped out their equipment. (*Gote House*)

A derelict RAF GCI bunker. The largest and perhaps most secret bunker in Sussex was created in 1942 as an extension to the Operation Aspidistra plan to infiltrate German domestic wavelengths. The massive bunker, on a 70-acre heathland site near Crowborough, took a Canadian Army road-building team and 600 civilian labourers three weeks to excavate. Triple shifts were worked, and the floodlights were only turned off if an air-raid threatened to expose the works. An illegal 500 kilowatt transmitter – the largest in the world at the time – was shipped over from the USA for use at the two-storey bunker. The operation took its name from the popular song 'The Greatest Aspidistra in the World', sung by Gracie Fields. (*Ted Awcock*)

Wartime hard-standings and a few mess-room Maycrete buildings remain at Brooklands, near Rye. The defunct RAF Rye domestic site is now used for fairs and market gatherings. (*Gote House*)

The popular *Dad's Army* characters take a break from filming at Seaford Head in 1970. (*Via Patricia Berry*)

DAD'S ARMY

Just as an Armoured Fighting Vehicle range dominated the terrain during the war, so the cliff-top meadows around Seaford Head have featured military life in postwar fiction. The opening scenes of David Lean's memorable, award-winning, 1952 film noir *The Sound Barrier* show the view across the English Channel from Hope Gap cliffs.

Of all the military television series screened, probably the most popular is the BBC's *Dad's Army*, which is generally reckoned to be more or less true to the wartime reality of the Home Guard volunteers. In September 1970 a production team from Columbia Pictures descended on Seaford Head with the fictional Walmington-on-Sea platoon for three days' filming. The opening scenes of the Columbia production showed credits super-imposed on old newsreel reports showing the murky English Channel and cliffs. Private Godfrey next emerged from a brick hut with the word GENTS on the door. (This building was in fact the now-demolished GPO Cable Sub-Station linking Hope Gap and France.) The closing scenes showed the platoon collectively agreeing that Herr Hitler and his generals had deferred their invasion plans once too often and that their Home Guard role was now over. *Dad's Army* has found a new generation of enthusiasts, who enjoy the entertaining comedy programme. The humour sometimes masks the truth of the situation during the early 1940s, when invasion was a real likelihood. The Dads Army Appreciation Society can be contacted via Jack Wheeler, 8 Sinuden Road, Wallingford, Oxfordshire OX10 8AA.

Known locally merely as 'the depository', this small storage unit existed unmarked for almost fifty years beside the B2192 on the Broyle out from Ringmer. Numerous similar installations were created by the Ministry of Agriculture and Fisheries as Cold War buffer storage depots in the late 1940s. (*Gote House*)

COLD WAR CONTINGENCIES

This once inconspicuous site at Ringmer, east of Lewes, was sealed off unsigned until the 1990s and was known locally only as a depository. Yet the Ministry specification buildings and security fences suggested a more serious application than civilian storage.

During the Cold War the Ministry of Agriculture, Fisheries and Food had buffer depots across the nation. This 1948 warehouse, adjacent to the B2192, was unit no. 347F of Butlers Wharf Ltd, which had corresponding installations in Kent and Surrey. The Free Trade Wharf Co. had similar storage facilities in Yorkshire while other installations across Britain were operated by Co-ordinated Traffic Services Ltd, Hays Wharf Ltd, New Fresh Wharf Co. Ltd and British and Foreign Wharf Co. Ltd among others. These depots held some of Britain's strategic food reserves.

The three postwar T2 hangars at Tangmere, on the 1940s Technical Site, were used as a grain store. They were later refurbished with ventilators, air-conditioning and humidity controls for storage of food stocks for the European Economic Community. Contingency planning remained a priority for the utility services, and regional town halls across Britain put together emergency relief plans as an extension of the 1940s ARP controls.

The Beachy Head single-level R1 Rotor bunker, built between 1949 and 1953, was surplus to RAF needs by 1957 and its contents were auctioned in April 1963. The Air Ministry was reluctant to release the site, which had been built at vast expense to house 200 key personnel in air-tight conditions. In the 1960s the Home Office Defence HQ in Forest Road, Tunbridge Wells, sought to adopt the bunker as a Civil Defence Control centre. In the 1980s plans to revitalise the bunker as a visitor attraction also came to naught and it has now been sealed off, the entrance buried.

With the passage of time most local crisis control centres became outdated, even if they were fully maintained. Typical examples can be identified in many towns and some continued to be activated, as with the 1992 Brede Water Works shelter. The ultimate county control centre was the underground Regional Seat of Government created at Kings Standing in the Ashdown Forest. This in turn was declared redundant in the mid-1980s and is currently occupied by the Sussex Police as a training facility.

In 1968 the Civil Defence structure was disbanded. Peace-time regional control by civil servants was abolished, but local authorities retained a role. The clerk acted as county controller and clerks of district councils as sub-controllers. An Emergency Defence Officer (later Emergency Officer) was appointed to coordinate local group activities of Emergency Volunteers.

SELECT TERMS & ABBREVIATIONS

AA	Anti-aircraft artillery.
ADGB	Air Defence of Great Britain.
AFC	Air Force Cross.
AI	Airborne Interception.
ALG	Advanced Landing Ground.
AMES	Air Ministry Experimental Station.
Anderson shelter	Arch-shaped corrugated-iron air-raid shelter, for civilian use.
Army track	Metal matting for construction of roadways.
ARP	Air Raid Precautions.
Bar and Rod	Runway base material comprising metal mesh-cast matting. See also Sommerfeld Track and Irving Grid.
Barbette mounting	Artillery mounting system whereby the gun is placed in an open pit, firing across a low wall or similar structure.
Battery (of guns)	A fixed defence artillery unit of up to eight guns.
BEF	British Expeditionary Force.
Bombing decoy	Dummy airfields, lighting, buildings and other sites to distract enemy from true sites. See also K site, Q site and Starfish.
BRC track	Reinforced runway surfacing.
Breech-loading gun	Guns loaded via their breech (as opposed to muzzle-loading) using a silk bagged charge.
Camouflage	Effective disguise or concealment of personnel, vehicles and structures, etc.
CH	Britain's secret Chain Home radar network developed from 1935 to great effect. The 360-ft-high metal transmitting masts and 240-ft-high wooden receiving masts were finally demolished in about 1960.
CHL	Chain Home Low radar was a beam-type radar rotating scan system providing low cover between main CH sites.
Circus	Bomber raids, supported by fighters, to provoke enemy responses.
Command post	Gunnery or operational control building.
Control tower	Airfield operations structure, usually sited on the perimeter of the airfield.

Dannert wire	Barbed wire rolls spread in concertina fashion.
Diver	V1 flying bomb deflection operations.
Domestic site	Personnel and servicing block site.
'Dragon's Teeth'	The popular name for the Ministry-designated 'pimples'. They were moulded concrete roadside markers or anti-tank restraints. They were also known as 'shark's teeth'.
Eagle	RAF squadrons consisting of American personnel.
ELG	Emergency Landing Ground.
Embrasure	An opening in a wall or pillbox, etc., for firing weapons. Also called a Loophole or Firing Loop.
ESCC	East Sussex County Council.
Engine room	Generator building.
FAA	Fleet Air Arm, transferred to Admiralty administration in 1939.
Fascine	Wooden bundles used for strengthening muddy roads and filling ditches, etc.
Filter room	Processing room wherein various reports were coordinated and analysed.
Firewatcher	Personnel positioned on upper storey of property to look out for and extinguish fires.
Firing loop	See embrasure.
Flak	German anti-aircraft gunfire, *Fliergerabwehrkannonen*.
Flame Fougasse	Inflammable drum concoction set in the ground to detonate with explosive charge.
Fougasse	Explosive charge of rock and metal objects set in the ground to deter enemy progress.
Foxhole	Small infantry trenches to accommodate one or two troops.
Friendly fire	Attack from one's own armed forces.
Gabion	Metal mesh or basket containers filled with stone or sand-bags providing temporary shelter.
GCI	Ground Controlled Interception.
Gun store	Storage for gun components.
HAA	Heavy anti-aircraft fire.
Hangar	Aircraft storage or servicing structures.
HE	High Explosive bombs.
Home Guard	Reconstituted from the Local Defence Volunteers on 14 July 1940.
ICBM	Intercontinental ballistic missile.
IRBM	Intermediate range ballistic missile.
Irving grid	Runway surface meshing for rapid installation.
K site	Day-time airfield decoy site.

LAA	Light anti-aircraft fire.
LDV	Local Defence Volunteers, formed 14 May 1940.
Limber	Vehicle trailer to carry ammunition.
Loophole	See embrasure.
Lyon light	A small and mobile type of electrically powered searchlight.
Machinery room	Naval term for electrical generator engine room.
Mess	Recreational and meals facility on a military camp.
MTB	Motor torpedo boat.
Muzzle-loading gun	Method of loading early guns via the muzzle.
NAAFI	Navy, Army and Air Force Institute.
Nissen hut	Second World War corrugated steel-framed buildings for various usages.
Nodal point	A community defended by road-blocks, pillboxes and Home Guard troops.
NRA	National Rivers Authority.
Operations room	Control centre for operational needs.
Orlit post	ROC observation post named after its originator and used after 1945.
Overhead cover	Protective roofing made of concrete or earth to protect occupants from the heat, flash and air burst of a nuclear explosion.
Parapet	Low protective walling.
Pedestal	Artillery mount.
Pillbox	Universal term from the First World War for mainland defence structures, named after Victorian pill-boxes because of their shape. Construction stopped in late 1940.
Plotting room	Operational map room for recording actions and incidents.
POW	Prisoner of War.
Predictor	Instrument developed to predict the range, height and position of aircraft.
Proximity fuse	Miniature radar-operated artillery fuse mechanism.
QL	Lighting decoy to resemble works, railways and towns.
Q site	Night-time airfield decoy site.
Quarters	Living accommodation.
Quick-firing gun (QF)	Breech-loaded gun using brass cartridges.
RAFA	Royal Air Force Association.
Ramrod	Day-time bomber raids with fighter escort.
Ranger	Deep penetration flights for targets of opportunity.
RDF	ReRadiation Direction Finding – early radar term.
Reinforced concrete	Concrete strengthened with steel rod or mesh inserts.
Revetment	Extra protection of emplacement using sand-bag or earth-filled supports.

RFC	Royal Flying Corps: formed on 13 April 1912 when King George V signed the Royal Warrant which brought the Corps into being. The RFC took over the former Air Battalion of the Royal Engineers. It became the RAF on 1 April 1918.
Rhubarb	Low-level strike over enemy-held territory.
Rifling	Spiral grooves in a gun barrel to rotate projectile.
RNAS	Royal Naval Air Service. On 3 September 1914 the RNAS was made responsible for British air defence.
RNVR	Royal Naval Volunteer Reserve.
Roadsted	Shipping attacks by Allied fighters.
ROC	Royal Observer Corps.
Rodeo	Fighter sweep.
Rotor	Integrated air defence network from 1949.
RSG	Regional Seat of Government.
Ryder flare	Illumination searchlight from pyrotechnic source.
Sangar	Stone breastworks, used as an alternative to trenches.
Seco hut	Accommodation units devised by Uni-Seco Structures Ltd.
Shuttering	Temporary lining of wood, corrugated iron or fabric to support concrete during setting.
Slit trench	Narrow trench universally adopted for troop protection.
Smooth-bore gun	Gun without rifling.
SOE	Special Operations Executive.
Sommerfeld track	Heavy steel netting held rigid by steel bars and rods, with edging and anchors, for runways and roads. Created by Kurt Sommerfeld, an expatriate Austrian, from First World War wire netting.
Sound mirror	Acoustic dish for detection of incoming aircraft.
SRSG	Sub-Regional Seat of Government.
Stand-by set house	RAF term for generator engine room construction.
Starfish	Urban bombing decoy site, also referred to as Special Fires or SF.
Technical site	Airfield allocation for support services, engineering and maintenance.
Temporary hutting	Ministry originated buildings designed for Second World War duration.
Turret	Enclosed structure in which a gun is mounted.
Utility	Standards established by government specialists for economic use of materials and constructions.
Vulnerable point	Specially guarded installation of war effort importance.
WAAF	Women's Auxiliary Air Force.
Watch office	Airfield operational buildings, later called Control Towers.
Weapon pit	Excavation in ground for artillery protection.
Y Service	British secret listening service.
Z battery	Unguided anti-aircraft rocket.

ACKNOWLEDGEMENTS

Sincere appreciation is extended to the many friends of old, and those made during the compilation of this book:

Stewart Angell, Ted Awcock, Peter Bailey, Steve Benz, Patricia Berry, Geoff Bridger, Patrick Burgess, David F. Cheshire, Peter Fellows, Martin Foster, John E. Goodwin, Michael Grainger, Les Green, Chris Horlock, Ron Martin, Roger Matthews, Michael Parrott, Joe Warr, John Wells and Phil Wooller.

Considerable care has been taken to secure permission to reproduce the illustrations in this compilation of county records. We have endeavoured to obtain agreement for any material still under copyright and apologise for any source not suitably cleared or acknowledged.

Notifying the publishers will ensure that future editions will include appropriate acknowledgements.

SOURCES AND FURTHER READING

Angell, Stewart. *The Secret Sussex Resistance*, Midhurst, Middleton Press, 1996
Ashdown Forest News
Barry Caine Archive
Beckett Newspapers Ltd
Black, Adam and Charles. *The Engines of War*, London, self-published, 1941
Brighton & Hove City Libraries
Chapman, Brigid. *People and Places of the High Weald, East Sussex*, Seaford, SB Publications, 1999
Ellis, Geoffrey. *The Secret Tunnels of South Heighton*, Seaford, SB Publications, 1996
d'Enno, D.C. *The Saltdean Story*, Chichester, Phillimore & Co. Ltd, 1985
East Sussex County Council Record Office, Lewes
East Sussex County Council Sites and Monuments Record
Georgano, G.N. *World War Two Military Vehicles*, London, Osprey Automotive, 1994
Greig, Ian, Leslie, Kim and Redman, Alan. *D-Day West Sussex*, Chichester, WSCC, 1994
McCarthy, Fiona and Dutton, E.P. *Eric Gill. A Lover's Quest for Art and God*, USA, Penguin, 1989
Moore, Judy. *Memories of Roedean*, Brighton, Roedean School, 1999
Newhaven Fort
Newhaven Local & Maritime Museum
Public Record Office, Kew
Ramsey, Winston G. *The Battle of Britain, Then and Now*, London, After the Battle Publications, 1989
St Dunstan's Archive, London
Sussex Industrial Archaeology Society
Swinfen, Warden and Arscott, David. *Hidden Sussex*, Brighton, BBC Radio Sussex, 1984
Webb, Commander E.D. *HMS Vernon – A Short History*, The Wardroom Mess, HMS *Vernon*, 1955
West Sussex County Council Record Office, Chichester

INDEX